IMAGES
of America

ANACAPA ISLAND

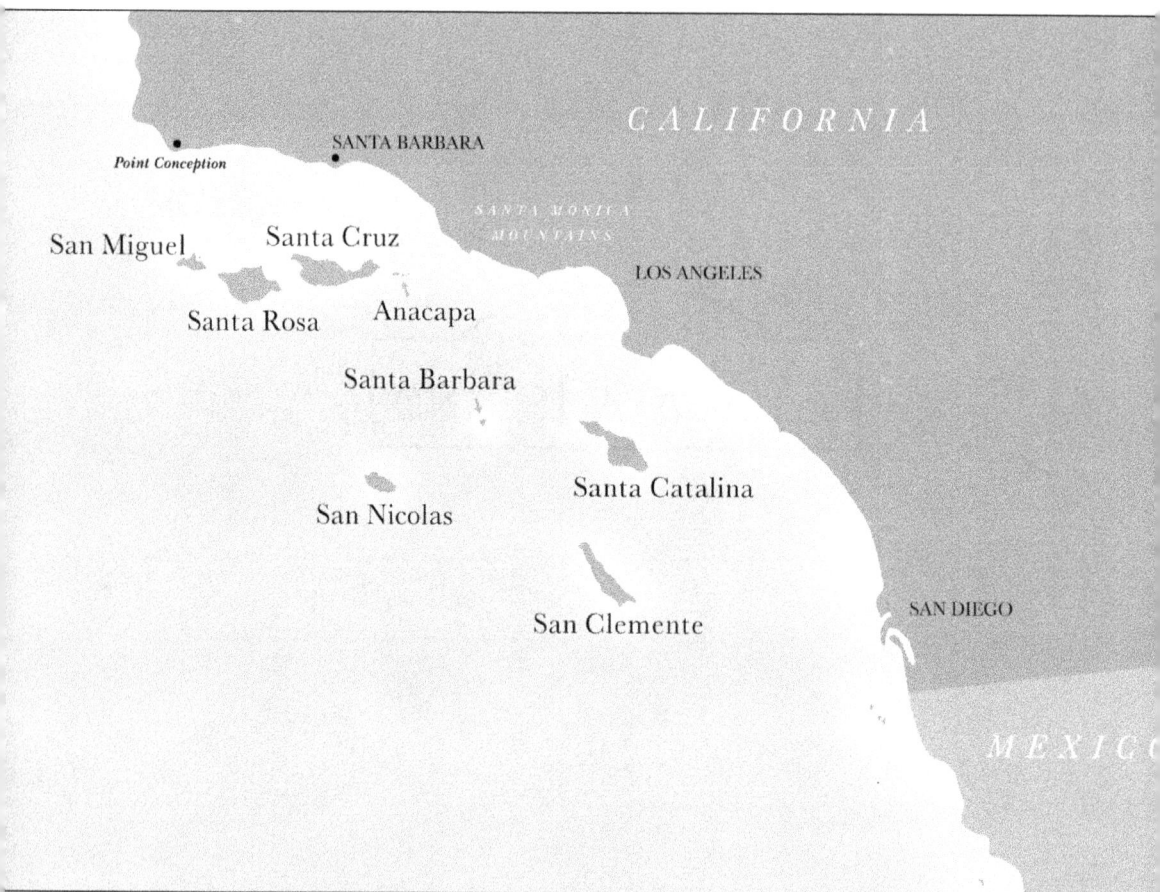

CALIFORNIA

Point Conception

SANTA BARBARA

San Miguel

Santa Cruz

SANTA MONICA MOUNTAINS

LOS ANGELES

Santa Rosa

Anacapa

Santa Barbara

Santa Catalina

San Nicolas

San Diego

San Clemente

MEXICO

ANACAPA ISLAND, ONE OF EIGHT CALIFORNIA CHANNEL ISLANDS. Eight California Channel Islands are located off the coast of Southern California, four northern and four southern. Anacapa Island is the easternmost and smallest of the four northern Channel Islands. Anacapa Island is composed of three separate islets: East, Middle, and West Anacapa Islands. (Santa Cruz Island Foundation.)

ON THE COVER: WAITING FOR A SAIL, MIDDLE ANACAPA ISLAND, 1889. In August 1889, a group of members of the Santa Barbara Natural History Society chartered Ezekiel Elliott's sloop *Brisk* for a 10-day cruise to Anacapa Island. The party included photographer Isaac Newton Cook (long beard) and his assistant Harry Jenkins (bowler hat), naturalist Lorenzo Yates (third from right), and Yates's good friend and noted artist Henry Chapman Ford (center, sitting in a chair). (Photograph by I.N. Cook; Santa Barbara Historical Museum.)

IMAGES

of America

ANACAPA ISLAND

Marla Daily
Santa Cruz Island Foundation

ARCADIA
PUBLISHING

Published by Arcadia Publishing
Charleston, South Carolina

Library of Congress Control Number: 2017963896

For all general information, please contact Arcadia Publishing:
Telephone 843-853-2070
Fax 843-853-0044
E-mail sales@arcadiapublishing.com
For customer service and orders:
Toll-Free 1-888-313-2665

Visit us on the Internet at www.arcadiapublishing.com

KIRK CONNALLY. Pictured here is Kirk Connally rowing his 15-foot Gloucester Gull dory along the south side of Santa Cruz Island. This book is dedicated to Connally, a master mariner, who introduced the author to many hidden treasures on Anacapa Island. (SCIF.)

CONTENTS

ACKNOWLEDGMENTS

This book was made possible by the Santa Cruz Island Foundation (SCIF), established by Carey Stanton (1923–1987) in 1985 to protect and preserve the cultural histories of all eight California Channel Islands. SCIF archives contain materials for all California Islands, and many of the images herein are from the SCIF collection. Warm thanks are due to the more than three dozen friends and photographers who shared their knowledge and island photographs, making this book possible: Kevin Bailey, Jeffrey Bozanic, Cherryl Connally, Bill Dewey, Bill and Nancy Ehorn, Dave Feliz, Holly Gellerman, Tom Haglund, Dan Harding, Tim Hauf, Richard Jackson, Steve Munch and Stephanie Hogue of Latitudes Fine Art Gallery, Nanci MacArthur, Doug Magnum, Don Mills (Meryl Allen Collection), Donna Mitnick, Lee Rentz, Jo Anne Sadler, Giancarlo Thomae, Jeanette Tonnies, Greg Webster, Jason and Jennifer Wendel, Robert "Flash" Wheeler, and Willie Wood. Dan Harding is singled out and applauded for sharing his many extraordinary Anacapa Island images taken over decades.

Invaluable assistance was also provided by personnel at many institutions: David Pereksta, Bureau of Ocean Energy Management (BOEM); Ann Huston, Laura Kirn, Derek Lohuis, and Yvonne Menard, Channel Islands National Park (CINP); Kathleen Correia, California State Library (CSL); Cherryl Connally, Island Packers Inc. (IPCO); Jim Dines, Los Angeles County Museum of Natural History (LACM); Los Angeles Public Library (LAPL); John Eaker, Library of Congress (LOC); Charles Johnson, Museum of Ventura County (MVC); Robert Schwemmer, National Oceanic and Atmospheric Administration (NOAA); Steve Junak and Randy Wright, Santa Barbara Botanic Garden (SBBG); Scott Zornig and Lynn Kubasek, Santa Barbara Channel Swimming Association (SBCSA); Michael Redmon, Santa Barbara Historical Museum (SBHM); Paul Collins, Santa Barbara Museum of Natural History (SBMNH); Greg Gorga, Santa Barbara Maritime Museum (SBMM); Millie Sunbear and Jaimie Jenks, Santa Cruz Island Foundation (SCIF); and Jill Thrasher, Sherman Library and Gardens (SL).

Most of all, I thank my extraordinary husband, Kirk Connally, for sharing his love of islands with me. Mil gracias to all!

INTRODUCTION

There is an intrinsic quality of mystery shared by islands throughout the world. What is on them? What is familiar? What is new and different? These questions naturally come to mind with each new island experience. Each of the eight California Channel Islands has its own heartbeat—its own unique combination of endemic, native, and introduced species—some shared in common with other islands, others not. Five of the eight islands fall within the boundaries of Channel Islands National Park, created by Congress in 1980: San Miguel, Santa Rosa, Santa Cruz, Anacapa, and Santa Barbara Islands. Public Law 96-99 calls for the protection of "the nationally significant natural, scenic, wildlife, marine, ecological, archaeological, cultural, and scientific values of the Channel Islands in the State of California." Park jurisdiction includes rocks, islets, submerged lands, and water within one nautical mile of each island. Permanent park headquarters and a visitor center are located at 1901 Spinnaker Drive in Ventura, California.

European explorers discovered the California Channel Islands in the 16th century. In 1542, Juan Rodríguez Cabrillo sailed among them with his ships *San Salvador* and *La Victoria*; Sir Francis Drake passed them aboard *Golden Hind* in 1579, and in 1595, Sebastián Rodríguez Cermeño visited several aboard the *San Agustín*. Only one 17th-century expedition left a written record of these islands—Sebastián Vizcaíno, who sailed to the West Coast of North America in 1602 with four vessels under orders of King Phillip of Spain. About 167 years later, Gaspar de Portolá's expedition of 1769 claimed the islands and all of Alta California for the king of Spain.

Anacapa Island was first named Santo Tomás by Juan Pérez, commander of the *San Antonio* in Portolá's 1769 Sacred Expedition. Two decades later, British navigator George Vancouver standardized the names of the eight California Channel Islands on his charts, applying the Chumash name "Enneecapah" to Anacapa Island, meaning ever-changing, or deception. Depending on the weather and approach to Anacapa, its three islets often appear as one large mesa or tableland. At other times, they are reflected in a mirage, making them appear much larger and closer.

In the 18th and 19th centuries, Spanish, English, Russian, and American sea captains hunted the channel waters in search of sea otters, valued for their pelts. As otter populations declined, scaling increased. Sealers inhabited Anacapa Island, primarily during the winter months when pinnipeds are more numerous, shooting seals and sea lions for their thick layers of blubber. The sealers rendered the blubber into oil in large try-pots, and an average seal could be expected to produce about a barrel of oil.

In 1821, with Mexico's successful revolt against Spain, the eight California Channel Islands passed from Spanish to Mexican ownership. The three largest islands were granted by Mexican governors of Alta California to private citizens. The other five islands remained un-granted: San Nicolas, San Clemente, San Miguel, Anacapa, and Santa Barbara Islands. The 1848 Treaty of Guadalupe Hidalgo ended the Mexican War in California, and Mexico ceded California to the United States. California statehood was granted by Pres. James K. Polk on September 9, 1850, and thus the California Channel Islands, including Anacapa Island, became a part of the state of California.

As US government property, the five un-granted islands served as transient homes to otter and seal hunters, Chinese and Japanese abalone fishermen, crawfishermen, smugglers, miners, and others seeking economic opportunity. In 1855, W.M. Johnson of the US Coast Survey reported:

> During the survey of Anacapa we were much delayed by fogs, which nearly enveloped the peak, on the top of which was one of my signals. Anacapa is a place of great resort for the seal, sea lion, and formerly the sea otter, but the latter have been all killed off for their fur. During the time we were surveying at Anacapa there was a small vessel engaged in seal hunting. The party consisted of five men; they had erected try-works on the north side of the middle island, at the top of the boat landing, and up to the time of landing had tried out eighty-five barrels of oil.

By 1875, seal oil was worth 35¢ to 45¢ a gallon, depending on its purity. The barrels of oil were sold for use in the manufacture of soap, leather, and cosmetics, and for burning in lamps. Ranchers also occupied the five smaller government-owned Channel Islands, first as squatters claiming possessory rights, then as official government lessees. Although ranching on an island was arduous work, those who undertook the enterprise seldom quit. The federal government issued a formal series of five-year leases to Anacapa Island beginning in 1902 and ending in 1937. Lessees included Louis LeMesnager (1902–1907), Heman Bayfield Webster (1907–1917), Ira Eaton (1917–1927), and Clarence Fay Chaffee (1932–1937); no lease was granted from 1927 to 1932. Provisions for private ranching on Anacapa Island terminated with the expiration of Chaffe's lease, which had only included Middle and West Anacapa Islands. East Anacapa had more important purposes.

In 1912, the US Lighthouse Service, also known as the Bureau of Lighthouses, turned on the first unmanned acetylene lantern on a 50-foot skeleton-tower on East Anacapa Island. It only required servicing twice a year. After a construction campaign of improvements in the early 1930s, the substantial Anacapa Island Lighthouse replaced the acetylene lantern. The light was turned on on March 25, 1932, and a series of lighthouse keepers were assigned to Anacapa Island duty. Seven years later, in 1939, the Bureau of Lighthouses was abolished, and its functions were turned over to the US Coast Guard.

By order of Pres. Franklin D. Roosevelt, Channel Islands National Monument was created in 1938, setting aside both Anacapa and Santa Barbara Islands, a status that remained until Pres. Jimmy Carter signed the authorization creating Channel Islands National Park in 1980.

Then as now, pleasure-seekers enjoy camping on the islands, walking their beaches, and hiking their hills. Public transportation to Channel Islands National Park (Anacapa, Santa Cruz, Santa Rosa, San Miguel, and Santa Barbara Islands) is available through park concessionaire Island Packers, which runs scheduled open-party boats to all five park islands. Private boaters may also land on all five park islands throughout the year. The trip to Anacapa Island offers the shortest boat ride—11 nautical miles—to the second smallest island—1.1 square miles in size. Once one has visited just one of the California Channel Islands, one will never look at them with the same eyes again.

One

OF CLIFFS AND CAVES

ANACAPA ISLAND LOOKING EAST. Anacapa Island lies in Ventura County, California, 4.5 miles to the west of Santa Cruz Island, Santa Barbara County. It is the second smallest of five islands in Channel Islands National Park, 1.1 square miles spread over a 5-mile length. At 930 feet in elevation, Summit Peak on West Anacapa Island is the highest point. Transportation for both day trips and camping is provided by park concessionaire Island Packers, serving the islands since 1968. (Photograph by Bill Dewey; SCIF.)

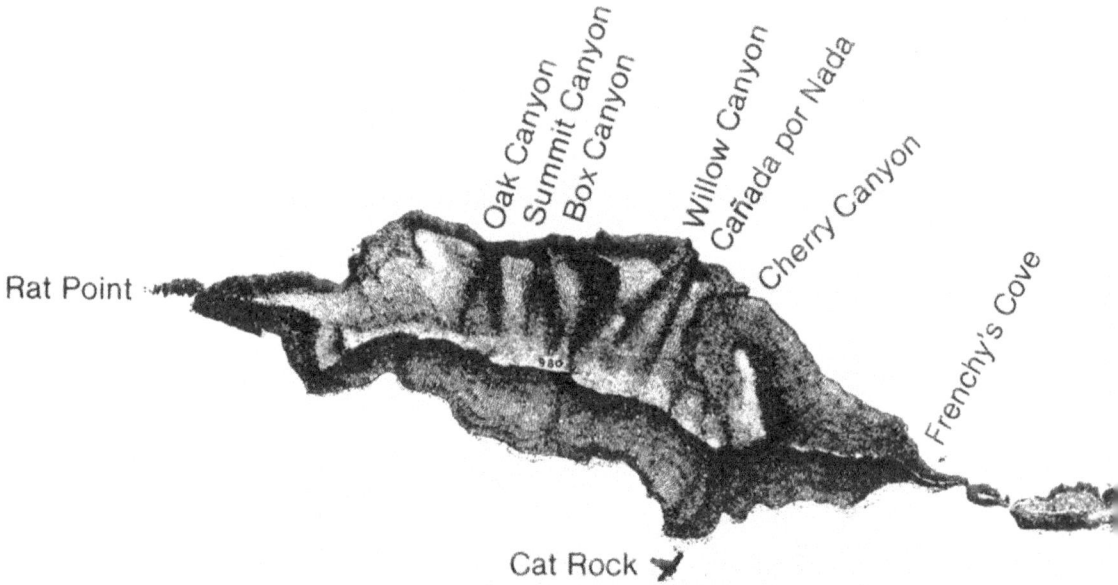

Oak Canyon
Summit Canyon
Box Canyon
Willow Canyon
Cañada por Nada
Cherry Canyon
Frenchy's Cove
Rat Point
Cat Rock

West Anacapa Island   **Middle**

Cathedral Cove

Landing Cove

Arch Rock

Shepherd's Cove

Sheep Camp

East Fish Camp

a Island

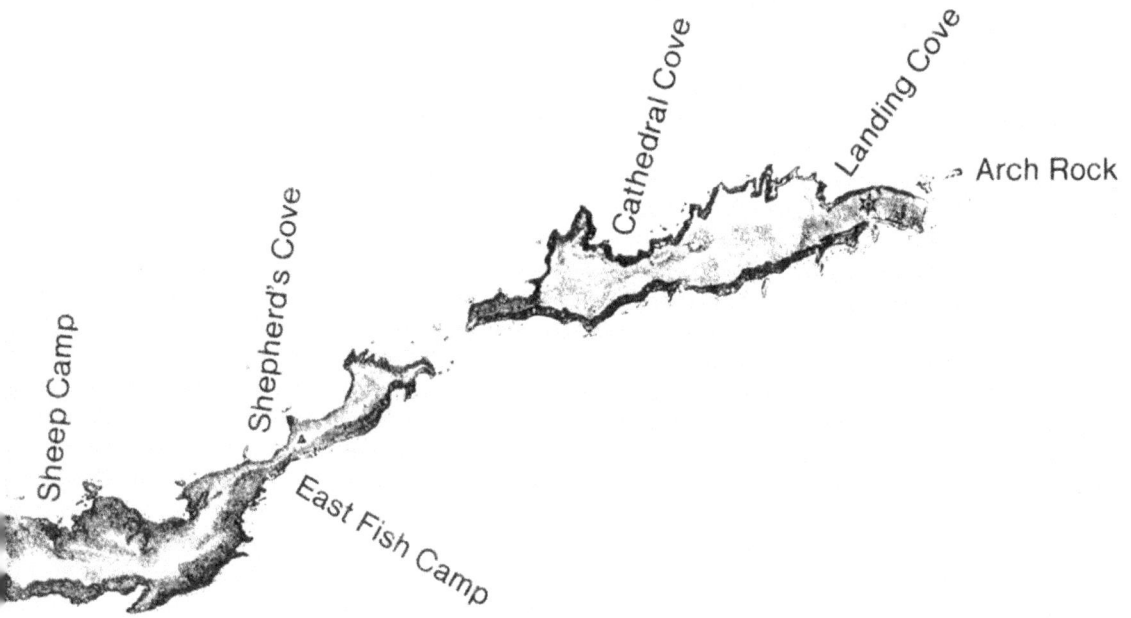

East Anacapa Island

MAP OF WEST, MIDDLE AND EAST ANACAPA ISLAND. Anacapa Island is the second smallest of the eight California Channel Islands. (SCIF.)

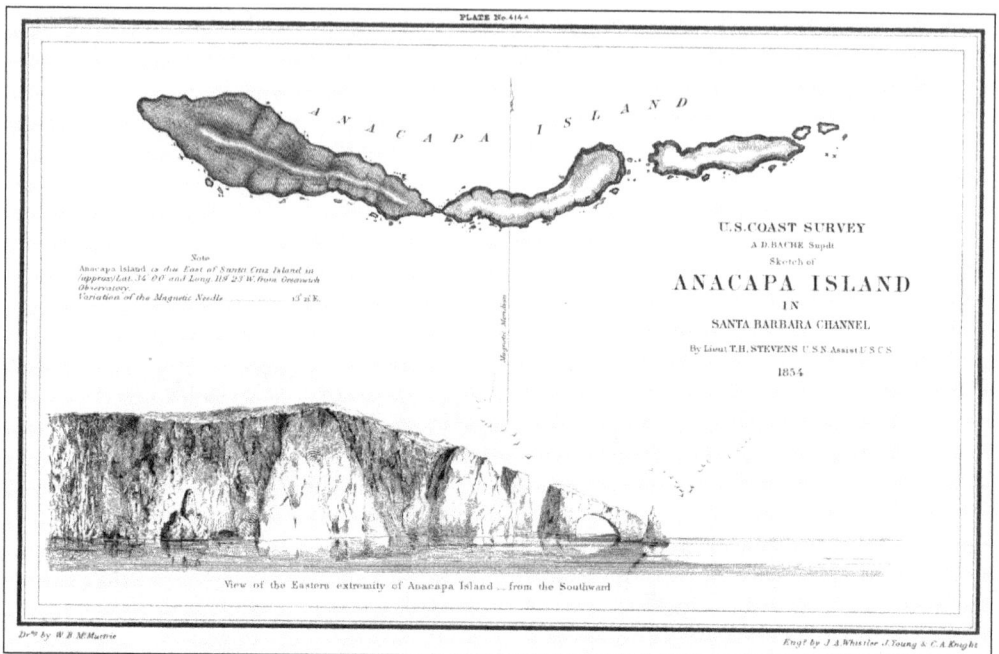

U.S. COAST SURVEY

A. D. BACHE Supdt

Sketch of

ANACAPA ISLAND

IN

SANTA BARBARA CHANNEL

By Lieut T.H. STEVENS U.S.N. Assist U.S.C.S

1854

View of the Eastern extremity of Anacapa Island ... from the Southward

WHISTLER'S VIEW OF EAST ANACAPA ISLAND. Artist James Abbott McNeil Whistler (1834–1903) was employed by the Coast Survey as a draftsman from November 1854 to February 1855. When tasked with preparing an engraving of Anacapa Island, Whistler added flocks of seagulls above Arch Rock. Criticized for taking such artistic license, he soon thereafter left his job. "Surely the birds don't detract from the sketch. Anacapa Island couldn't look as blank as that map did before I added the birds," he famously responded. In 1856, the map was reprinted without the birds. In 1871, Whistler painted his celebrated *Arrangement in Grey and Black, No. 1* (known as "Whistler's Mother"). (SCIF.)

ARCH ROCK WITH ISLAND PACKERS CATAMARAN ISLANDER, EAST ANACAPA ISLAND. The 40-foot-high natural bridge off the east end of East Anacapa is the island's most iconic and prominent feature. (SCIF.)

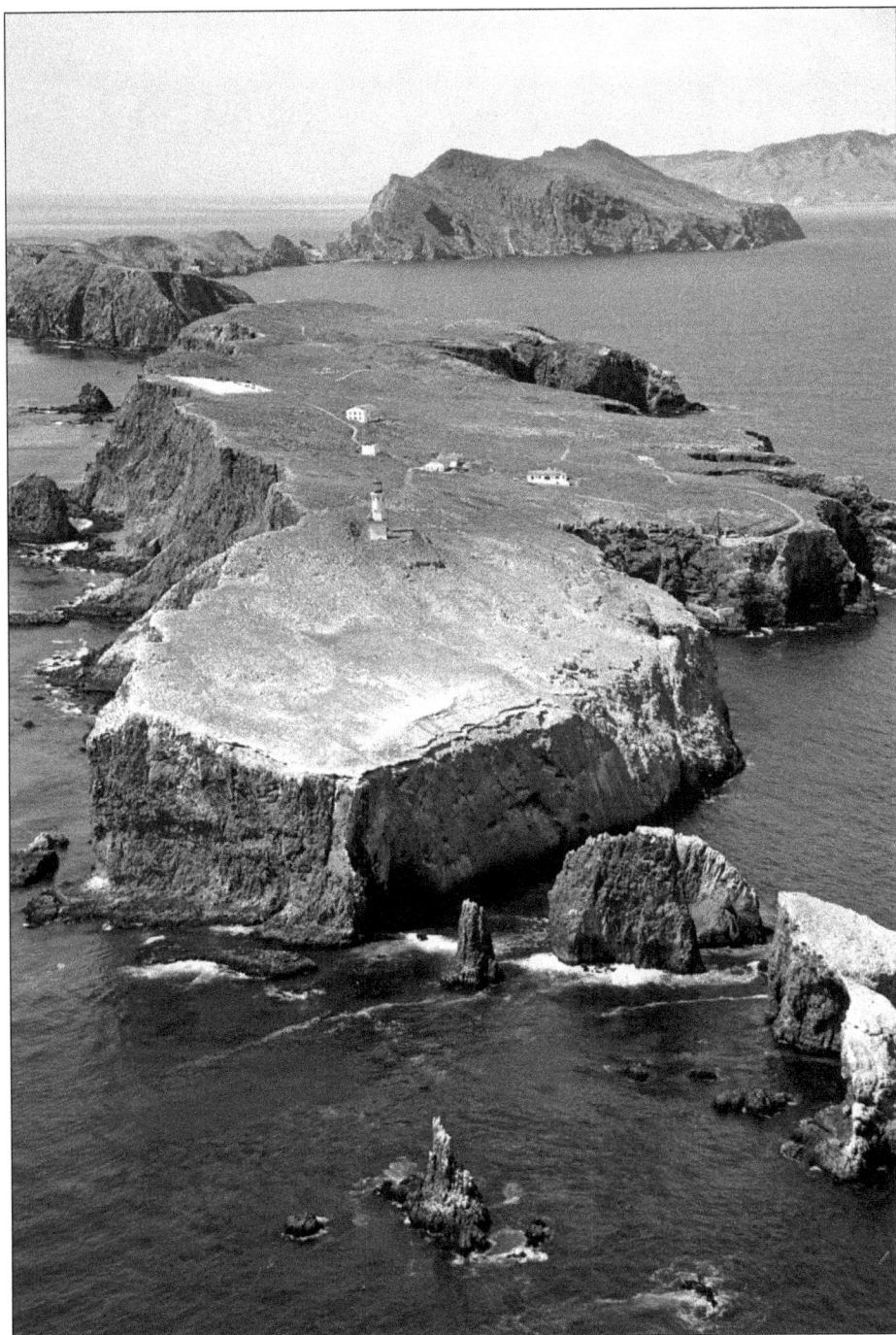

AERIAL VIEW LOOKING WEST, EAST ANACAPA ISLAND. East Anacapa is the smallest of the three islets, a cliff island rising from the sea as a seemingly inaccessible mesa. The slightly terraced top of approximately 100 acres lies about 200 feet above sea level. Its highest point reaches 250 feet at the base of the lighthouse. Facilities on East Anacapa include the 50-foot-tall lighthouse, fog signal, multiple park service buildings, a well-marked nature trail, and a public campground. (Photograph by Dan Harding.)

ARCH ROCK REFLECTED IN A CALM SEA, EAST ANACAPA ISLAND. Calm sea states at Anacapa Island are a kayaker's dream. There are two through-tunnels on each side of Arch Rock, each with two entrances, which can be explored by kayak. The cave to the left (east) of the arch is actually a 23-foot-high, 93-foot-long tunnel that varies from 8 to 12 feet wide. It comes out into the arch. (Photograph by Dan Harding.)

LANDING COVE, EAST ANACAPA ISLAND. The only access to the top of the mesa is from Landing Cove on the island's north side. This small inlet is bounded by vertical cliffs on all sides. On the west edge of the inlet, an elevated dock is built into the cliff side from which a series of 157 concrete and metal steps switch back vertically to the top of the island. (Photograph by Dan Harding.)

ISLAND PACKERS CATAMARAN *ISLAND ADVENTURE* AT ENTRANCE TO LANDING COVE, EAST ANACAPA ISLAND. Waves and wind have eroded this five-mile-long volcanic spine into three islets with towering sea cliffs, caves, and natural bridges. The Anacapa Island Lighthouse and fog signal are above Landing Cove at an elevation of 277 feet. (Photograph by Dan Harding.)

LANDING COVE STAIRS DELIVERY, EAST ANACAPA ISLAND, 2010. The old steel staircase embedded into the 150-foot cliff at Landing Cove was badly eroded by the sea air. It was replaced with a new one, delivered in sections by a Sikorsky S-64 Skycrane helicopter. Installing the stairs was an engineering challenge. The island was closed for more than six months (June–December 2010) for the replacement project. (SCIF.)

LADDER AND STAIR ACCESS TO EAST ANACAPA ISLAND. From the vessel, all arriving and departing visitors climb or descend a vertical ladder connected to a lower landing platform embedded into the cliff face. Island Packers maneuvers its vessel against the pilings, holding the vessel in place while passengers offload or load. During high swells and seas, landings at East Anacapa Island are not possible. (Photograph © 2012 by Lee H. Rentz.)

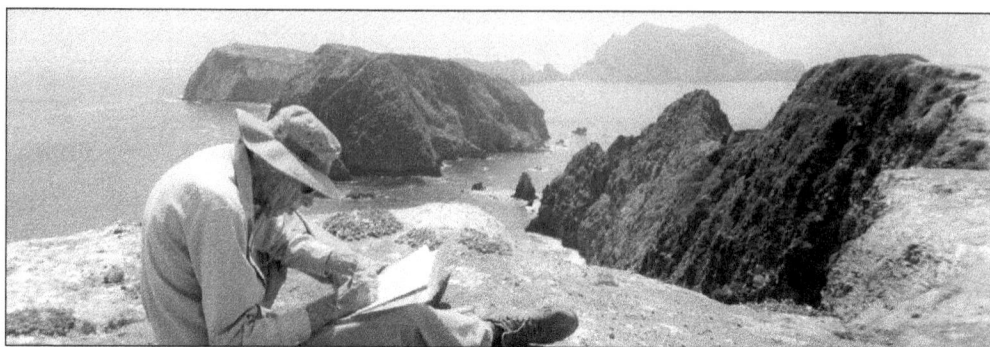

LEGENDARY GEOLOGIST TOM DIBBLEE MAPPING THE ANACAPAS, 1998. Anacapa Island is predominantly volcanic in origin, composed of highly weathered Miocene volcanic rock that has been eroded by wind and waves. In a few locations, sedimentary rocks can be found, including the blue-green San Onofre breccia on the south shore of West Anacapa near Cat Rock. Many submarine lava flows can be seen on the island. Fissures forming sea caves and blowholes are common. (Photograph by William Wood; SCIF.)

CATHEDRAL COVE, EAST ANACAPA ISLAND. Cathedral Cove is located on the north side of East Anacapa Island to the west of Landing Cove. Multiple caves line the cove, including Cathedral Cave. Cathedral Arch, passable in a kayak on calm days, connects the cove with a small cove just to the west where three of the five entrances to Cathedral Cave are located. (Photograph by Dan Harding.)

EAST ANACAPA ISLAND FACING WEST. Fog provides much needed moisture to the vegetation on an otherwise waterless Anacapa Island, home of a large colony of western gulls. (Photograph by Dan Harding.)

THE GAP BETWEEN EAST AND MIDDLE ANACAPA ISLETS. The gap between East and Middle Anacapa Islets is easily viewed from Inspiration Point atop East Anacapa Island. At low tide, most of the land between the two islets is exposed. Visitors are allowed on Middle Anacapa by permit only. (Photograph by Marla Daily; SCIF.)

KEYHOLE ROCK AND CAVE, MIDDLE ANACAPA ISLAND. A 100-foot-high rock arch, shaped like a keyhole, protrudes prominently from the north shore of Middle Anacapa Island to the west of Sheep Camp. Directly adjacent (west) of the rock feature is an unusual two-level cave that extends 590 feet into the island. The upper level is dry before it drops some 18 feet to the lower level, accessible only at low tide. (Photograph by Marla Daily; SCIF.)

FRENCHY'S CAVE (YATES' CAVE), WEST ANACAPA ISLAND, 1970. Some 45 tidal and sea caves are found along the shores of West Anacapa Island: 31 along the north shore and another 14 along the south shore. Frenchy's Cave, located 2,000 feet west of Frenchy's Cove, is 421 feet deep, and is the most spacious of the caves found on West Anacapa Island. It can be explored by dinghy or kayak. During Prohibition, island resident Raymond "Frenchy" LeDreau stored bootleg liquor in the cave. (Photograph by E. Bruce Howell; LAPL.)

FRENCHY'S COVE, WEST ANACAPA ISLAND. West Anacapa is the largest, highest, and most topographically diverse of the three islets. Summit Peak reaches 930 feet in elevation. Visitation is limited to Frenchy's Cove and tide-pool areas due to pelican and seabird nesting activity. This small but accessible stretch of cobblestone beach, 200 feet long, offers the best landing on all three islets. A narrow sea channel separates it from Middle Anacapa Island. Formerly named Webster Bay for island lessee H. Bay Webster, the name changed to Frenchy's Cove once fisherman Raymond "Frenchy" LeDreau established camp here. (Photograph by Dan Harding.)

21

INDIAN SPRING CAVE, WEST ANACAPA ISLAND. A rare source of fresh water, Indian Spring Cave is only 300 feet west of Frenchy's Cave. In 1890, Lorenzo Yates noted that a rare freshwater seep inside this cave produced 70 gallons of fresh water every 24 hours. In the 20th century, anthropologist John Harrington interviewed Fernando Librado, a Mission San Buenaventura Indian, who told Harrington that the Chumash used water seepage from this cave. This photograph of botanist Ralph Philbrick (1934–2017) was taken in 1979. (Photograph by Steve Junak; SBBG.)

Two

SEALERS, SHEEPMEN, AND PLEASURE-SEEKERS

SEALERS ON ANACAPA ISLAND. With California statehood in 1850, Anacapa Island became US government property. In 1854, it was set aside for lighthouse purposes, but until 1902, Uncle Sam took little interest in the island or its occupants. Beginning in the latter half of the 19th century, English, Russian, and American sea captains combed the kelp beds off the Channel Islands in search of sea otters, hunted for their valuable pelts. As the otters disappeared, sealers killed seals and sea lions for their blubber, which was tried into oil. (Photograph by I.N. Cook; SBHM.)

23

VIEW OF MIDDLE ANACAPA ISLAND, 1889. Middle Anacapa, the second largest of the three islets, is a little over three miles long, but seldom over one-eighth of a mile wide. It rises to 325 feet in elevation. A camp and anchored sailboat can be seen in the distance at left. (Photograph by I.N. Cook; SBHM.)

MIDDLE ANACAPA ISLAND LOOKING EAST, 1889. Landing on Middle Anacapa is possible on the north shore near the middle of the island at Sheep Camp. Today, however, Middle Anacapa Island is closed to the public. It is set aside for the island wildlife. A small grove of eucalyptus trees marks the site of former ranch buildings. (Photograph by I.N. Cook; SBHM.)

24

NORTH SHORE OF THE ANACAPAS FACING WEST, 1889. Throughout the last half of the 19th century, Anacapa Island remained a busy little island, where sealers captured their prey, fishermen worked the surrounding offshore waters, lobstermen trapped crawfish in nearshore waters, and Chinese gathered abalone along the rocky shoreline. Campers and pleasure-seekers ventured to Anacapa to gather seaweeds and shells and explore its many caves. (Photograph by I.N. Cook; SBHM.)

ELLIOTT'S HARBOR, MIDDLE ANACAPA ISLAND, AS SEEN FROM THE SLOOP, 1889. In the 19th century, a succession of men with sheep-ranching interests squatted on Anacapa Island, using it to raise and graze sheep, selling what interests they could to others as they left. In 1869, William Dover filed a quitclaim deed to Anacapa Island, an investment he then sold to Louis Burgert and Warren H. Mills. They in turn transferred island interests to the Pacific Wool Growing Company. (Photograph by I.N. Cook; SBHM.)

ELLIOTT'S SHEEP CAMP ON MIDDLE ANACAPA ISLAND, 1889. Early sheep ranchers developed Middle Anacapa Island as their base of operations. Several building pads were leveled on the slope above a small landing cove area. In 1875–1876, Anacapa Island appeared on the delinquent tax list for nonpayment of state and county taxes in the county of Ventura. The list of assets on the island included 3,000 improved sheep with a value of $6,000, and 400 lambs valued at $400. (Photograph by I.N. Cook; SBHM.)

EARLY VIEW OF ELLIOTT'S SHEEP CAMP, MIDDLE ANACAPA ISLAND, 1889. In 1882, Ezekiel Elliott (1833–1912) and his son Joseph Vincent Elliott (1860–1943) bought the rights to Anacapa Island from the Pacific Wool Growing Company. They ran sheep on the island for 16 years (1882–1897). In 1897, they sold their Anacapa interests to Frenchman Louis LeMesnager for $8,000. In 1902, these possessory interests stopped when the government instituted a formal lease agreement policy. Note the eucalyptus trees. (Photograph by I.N. Cook; SBHM.)

ELLIOTT'S RANCH BUILDINGS, MIDDLE ANACAPA ISLAND, 1889. The Santa Barbara *Daily Independent* of August 16, 1889, included this report: "There are some good buildings on the middle island which Mr. Elliott kindly permitted us to occupy, and during our stay we lived high and slept higher, having to climb some distance to get to the dining room adjoining the kitchen, which last, was located out of doors; and for sleeping we had to climb still higher to the upper building which is perhaps 150 feet or more above tide water, and from the veranda a magnificent view across the channel." (Photograph by I.N. Cook; SBHM.)

WAITING FOR A SAIL, MIDDLE ANACAPA ISLAND, 1889. With gear packed, members of the Santa Barbara Natural History Society camping party await their chartered sloop, *Brisk.* Artist Henry Chapman Ford (seated at center), naturalist Lorenzo Yates (third from right), and photographer I.N. Cook (long beard) were among the adventurers. (Photograph by I.N. Cook; SBHM.)

ARTIST H.C. FORD OUTSIDE A CAVE ON ANACAPA ISLAND, 1889. Artist Henry Chapman Ford (1828–1894) moved to Santa Barbara in 1875, where he was one of the original founders of the Santa Barbara Natural History Society in 1876 with his close friend Lorenzo Yates. Ford was interested in archaeology, botany, and geology. Here, he is seen on Anacapa Island with his sketchbook to the right of a cave entrance. (Photograph by I.N. Cook; SBHM.)

MORNING AT THE ANACAPAS BY HENRY CHAPMAN FORD, 1888. This painting of the gap between East and Middle Anacapa Islands by H.C. Ford was selected by John Muir as one of several used to illustrate his book *Picturesque California*, published in 1888. The location of the original painting is unknown. (SCIF.)

CAMP GIDNEY, MIDDLE ANACAPA ISLAND, AUGUST 1890. Southern California historian Charles M. Gidney (1855–1933), author of *History of Santa Barbara, San Luis Obispo and Ventura Counties* (published in 1917), participated in a large camping party on Middle Anacapa Island in 1890. Gidney took his wife, Clara, and their three-and-a-half-year-old son, Ray, on the trip. (SBHM.)

GIDNEY PARTY ON MIDDLE ANACAPA ISLAND, AUGUST 1890. The Santa Barbara *Daily Independent* of August 21, 1890, reported: "The party of nineteen, who visited the islands of Santa Cruz and Anacapa last week, speak in high terms of their trip and join in recommending a similar one to parties who desire a first class time at a very reasonable expense. The scenery on and around the islands, the wonderful arches and mysterious caves, the exquisite beauty of sky and ocean at morning and evening above all the delightful and invigorating temper of the climate, make the place of rare interest to the health or pleasure seeker." (SBHM.)

GIDNEY PARTY GATHERED ON MIDDLE ANACAPA ISLAND, AUGUST 1890. Santa Barbara surveyor Frank Flournoy (1868–1960) and his wife, Nellie, were among the large group of friends who camped at Middle Anacapa Island. From left to right are Minnie Jennings, Edith McGrath, Mrs. Flournoy, May Washburn, and Miss Weaver. (SBHM.)

GAP BETWEEN MIDDLE AND WEST ANACAPA ISLAND. A surge channel divides Middle and West Anacapa. The gap and its tide pools can be explored on foot during low tides. West Anacapa Island is closed to the public, except at Frenchy's Cove and the accessible connected tide pools on the island's south side. (Photograph by I.N. Cook; SBHM.)

CAMPING ON WEST ANACAPA ISLAND, 1895. Photographer John Calvin Brewster (1841–1909) chronicled life in Ventura County from 1874—a year after its founding—until his death in 1909. The rare images he captured, including this one of a camp at Frenchy's Cove on West Anacapa Island in 1895, are preserved in his original glass-plate negatives at the Museum of Ventura County. (SCIF.)

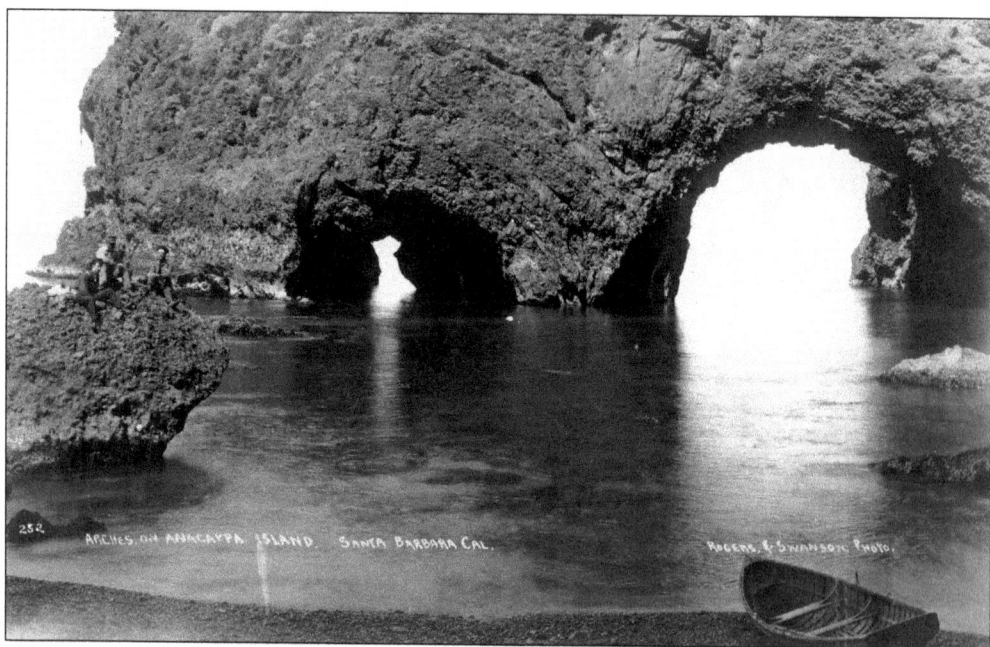

TWIN ARCH, WEST ANACAPA ISLAND, C. 1898. At the east end of Frenchy's Cove, near the gap that separates Middle and West Anacapa Islands, is a small pocket beach bounded by a large twin arch. The arches can be traversed during calm seas at low tide. (Photograph by Rogers & Swanson; CSL.)

FORMER LAND BRIDGE, WEST ANACAPA ISLAND. At the eastern end of Frenchy's Cove on West Anacapa Island, a land bridge with a footpath on it once spanned an arched gap. Cabins were built on either side. After the natural bridge collapsed, it was replaced with a wooden bridge. That too eventually washed away. (MVC.)

YATES' CAVE, WEST ANACAPA ISLAND, 1890. Yates Cave, located 2,000 feet west of Frenchy's Cove, is the most spacious and second-deepest of the 45 caves found on West Anacapa Island. It was originally described by Santa Barbara naturalist Lorenzo Yates (1837–1909) in the January 1890 issue of *American Geologist*. Sometime after 1928, the cave's name was changed by popular use to Frenchy's Cave. (LAPL.)

YATES' CAVE INTERIOR, WEST ANACAPA ISLAND, 1890. Past the water entrance to this 420-foot-deep cave are two areas of cobble beach backed by a sandy slope. During Prohibition, island resident Raymond "Frenchy" LeDreau allegedly stored bootleg liquor in the cave. (SBHM.)

INDIAN SPRING CAVE, WEST ANACAPA ISLAND, C. 1889. Within this dry, 100-foot-deep cave, located 300 feet west of Yates' (Frenchy's) Cave, a spring of good water seeps from the rocks. Native American islanders collected water from this cave, as did later Anacapa Island occupants in the late 19th and early 20th centuries. Note the people inside. (Photograph by I.N. Cook; SBHM.)

PLEASURE-SEEKERS PICNICKING ON WEST ANACAPA ISLAND. Anacapa Island served as a destination for day-trippers and campers in the late 19th and early 20th centuries. (MVC.)

FRENCHMAN GEORGE LEMESNAGER. George LeMesnager (1850–1923) arrived in Los Angeles in 1866. He indulged in multiple business interests, including paying Ezekiel Elliott $8,000 in gold coin for his interests on Anacapa Island in 1897. These included several buildings on Middle Anacapa Island and the island's sheep. His 19th-century interests were the last to be purchased prior to the US government initiating an official lease policy for Anacapa Island beginning in 1902. (LOC.)

Three

Lessees, Frenchy, and an Erstwhile Mayor

The Mesa atop Middle Anacapa Island, 1940. The first Anacapa Island lease (1902–1907) was awarded to Louis LeMesnager. In 1897, his father, Frenchman George LeMesnager, had paid Ezekiel Elliott $8,000 in gold coin for his Anacapa Island interests. In 1902, the Lighthouse Service instituted a formal leasing program for Anacapa Island, and Louis LeMesnager (1876–1957) was granted the first five-year lease for a term of five years at an annual rental of $5. (Photograph by Don Meadows; SL.)

MARTHA AND HEMAN BAYFIELD "BAY" WEBSTER. The second and third Anacapa Island leases (1907–1917) were awarded to Bay Webster. In 1907, Webster (1870–1950) became the second Anacapa Island lessee, bidding $31 a year for five years. He paid previous lessee Louis LeMesnager for 40 to 50 sheep already on the island, and purchased another 250 sheep from the neighboring Santa Cruz Island. Webster was known as the "King of Anacapa Island." (Greg Webster; SCIF.)

HEMAN BAYFIELD WEBSTER AND FAMILY, WEST ANACAPA ISLAND, C. 1910. Bay Webster (back right), his wife Martha (far right), and sons Morris (front) and Harvey raised sheep and catered to fishermen and tourists on Anacapa Island. For the 1911 school year, a governess/tutor was brought out for the Webster boys, and Anacapa Island's temporary school took place in a tent. (SCIF.)

HARVEY WEBSTER AT WEBSTER BAY, WEST ANACAPA ISLAND, C. 1914. Harvey Brackett Webster (1904–1977) was the younger of two sons of H. Bay and Martha Webster. His father had the lease on Anacapa Island for 10 years (1907–1917). (MVC.)

H. Bay Webster's boat Anacapa, c. 1911. *Anacapa* (No. 204874) was a 35-foot motor launch built in Everett, Washington, in 1906. She had a two-cylinder gas engine. During the years Webster had the Anacapa Island lease, he advertised daylight or moonlight camping excursions aboard his appropriately-named vessel. The *Anacapa* was in service until at least 1917. (MVC.)

APPROACH FROM THE MAINLAND, MIDDLE ANACAPA ISLAND. When H. Bay Webster obtained his first of two five-year leases for Anacapa Island in 1907, a number of wooden buildings existed on Middle Anacapa Island that had served as headquarters for prior sheep ranchers dating to the mid-1880s. Introduced eucalyptus trees surrounded some of the buildings. (MVC.)

H. BAY WEBSTER AT THE SKIFF HOIST, MIDDLE ANACAPA ISLAND. In addition to several wooden buildings on Middle Anacapa Island, there was a hoist used to lift small skiffs out of the water at the dubious rocky landing. (MVC.)

SHEEP CHUTE, MIDDLE ANACAPA ISLAND. Sheep were placed on Anacapa Island in the early 1870s and raised by a series of squatting ranchers and island lessees. To get sheep off the island, they were hog-tied and slid down a wooden chute, then loaded onto a waiting vessel. (MVC.)

H. Bay Webster and Isa Strathern, Middle Anacapa Island, c. 1915. By the time Bay Webster got the lease on Anacapa Island (1907–1917), the buildings on Middle Anacapa Island were decades old, dating to the Elliott era of the 1880s. (Photograph by Charles Stanton; SBMM.)

Webster's Camp at Webster Bay, West Anacapa Island, c. 1910. In addition to raising sheep on Anacapa Island, H. Bay Webster catered to pleasure-seekers, day-trippers, and campers. He also provided transportation to and from the island aboard his vessel *Anacapa*. (SBMM.)

WEBSTER BAY, WEST ANACAPA ISLAND. Webster built five shacks on West Anacapa Island: Capacity, Felicity, Simplicity, Intensity, and Necessity (the outhouse). Building sites were leveled along the eastern end of the islet at the only suitable landing beach, renamed Frenchy's Cove after 1928. The cabins were connected by a footpath and bridge. (MVC.)

POSTCARD OF WEBSTER BAY, WEST ANACAPA ISLAND, C. 1915. When Webster's five-year lease ended in 1912, five men bid for the next five-year lease, from 1912–1917. H. Bay Webster won it again, this time with his high bid of $381 a year for five years, just 75¢ higher than Capt. Ira K. Eaton's bid. This new lease was only for Middle and West Anacapa Island, since a light had been installed on East Anacapa by the Lighthouse Service in 1912. (SCIF.)

WOODEN BRIDGE, WEST ANACAPA ISLAND. A natural bridge arch and footpath originally connected several of the cabins at the east end of Webster Bay (see page 33). After it collapsed, the span was replaced by a wooden bridge. With time, the wooden bridge was lost. (CINP.)

Ira K. Eaton. The fourth and fifth Anacapa Island leases (1917–1927) were awarded to Capt. Ira K. Eaton, seen here at the wheel. Eaton (1876–1938) ran a resort at Pelican Bay on neighboring Santa Cruz Island for 27 years. During this time, he also leased Anacapa Island from the federal government, paying $607.50 a year for his first lease. He used the island to support fish camps and graze sheep. (SCIF.)

Ira Eaton's Sheep, Middle Anacapa Island, 1917. In addition to raising sheep, Eaton was well known for his rum-running prowess, and during Prohibition he used Anacapa Island as a storage place for bootlegged liquor. His Anacapa Island lease fees were in part paid by the Larco brothers, who placed fishermen on Anacapa Island. When his second lease expired in 1927, no lease was issued for the next five-year period (1927–1932). (SCIF.)

CLARENCE FAY CHAFFEE. The sixth and last Anacapa Island lease (1932–1937) was awarded to Ventura businessman C.F. Chaffee (1889–1979). His high bid was $760 a year for five years. His interest was in developing a sport-fishing camp. Chaffee took in partners Al Derby, Meryl Allen, and a Mr. Philbrick for the venture, but the elaborate plans never came to fruition. Chaffe's was the last lease issued by the federal government for Anacapa Island. (Nanci Macarthur.)

RAYMOND "FRENCHY" LEDREAU, C. 1940. Legendary fisherman Raymond "Frenchy" LeDreau (1875–1962) moved to West Anacapa Island sometime around 1928 and stayed for six years the first time. In 1934, Frenchy moved to neighboring Santa Cruz Island until 1938, when he returned to Anacapa Island for an additional 20 years. (Merrill Carr Allyn Collection; Don Mills.)

FISHERMAN CHARLES JOHNSON, C. 1873–1938. When Frenchy moved off West Anacapa Island in 1934, the vacancy was filled by "Old Swede" Charles Johnson, until his death in his cabin in September 1938. For four years, Johnson was known as the erstwhile mayor of Anacapa Island. Johnson boasted he had received a dishonorable discharge from the Navy for talking back to Admiral Dewey. (Meryl Carr Allen Collection; Don Mills.)

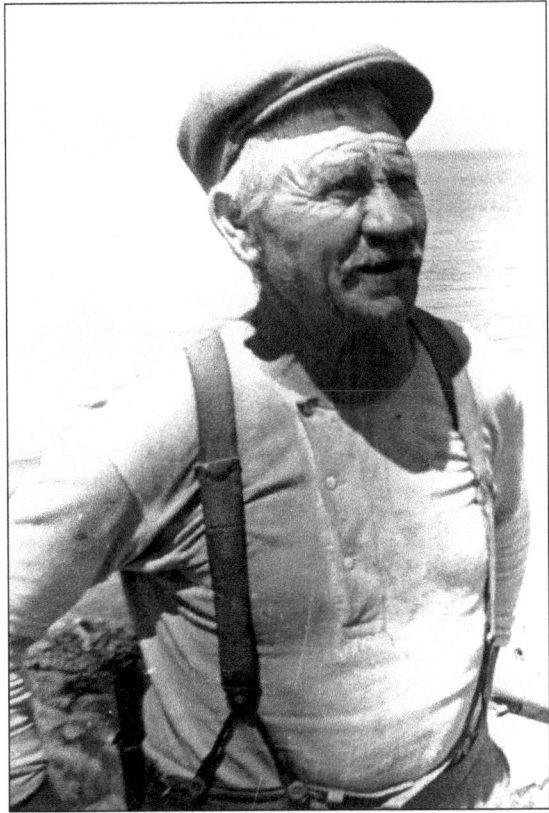

CHARLES JOHNSON AT ANACAPA ISLAND, C. 1936. According to Merrill Allyn, Johnson never failed to take a bath on his birthday (October 12), Columbus Day, Christmas, and certain other occasions. After his last trip to town in 1938, a fellow fisherman dropped him off on Anacapa Island. "Charley climbed the path to his island home, went in, closed the door, lay down on his bed and died—just like he said he wanted to do." (Meryl Carr Allen Collection; Don Mills.)

FRENCHY AND HIS DAY'S CATCH, WEST ANACAPA ISLAND, 1939. Frenchy lived alone with his many cats in one of several cabins at the cove that now bears his name. From a tiny window in his cabin, Frenchy could see steamers and potential visitors passing by. He often traded lobster or fish for necessary supplies and liquor. (CINP.)

FRENCHY LEDREAU AND BAY WEBSTER, WEST ANACAPA ISLAND, C. 1940. When he was about 70, former Anacapa Island lessee H. Bay Webster (right) paid a visit to current island resident Frenchy LeDreau. Webster spent 10 years (1907–1917) at Anacapa Island; Frenchy spent 26 years (1928–1954, with a four-year absence). Over time, the name of the beach on West Anacapa Island changed from Webster Bay to Frenchy's Cove. (CINP.)

FRENCHY'S COVE, WEST ANACAPA ISLAND, C. 1950S. A narrow trail led from Frenchy's shack to the beach where he kept his lobster traps, fishing gear, and mooring device for pulling his skiff above high water. Behind Frenchy's Cove, Summit Peak rises to 930 feet. (CINP.)

FRENCHY'S CAMP, WEST ANACAPA ISLAND, C. 1948. Frenchy built, repaired, and stored his lobster traps above the high tide line on the beach below the shack he occupied for more than two decades. (Meryl Carr Allen Collection; Don Mills.)

OFFSHORE VIEW OF FRENCHY'S CAMP, WEST ANACAPA ISLAND, C. 1948. Frenchy was alone on Anacapa Island for weeks at a time. Described as a "hermit who enjoyed company," he welcomed the opportunity of having visitors stop and pay a visit. Many left him with food, drink, and supplies. (Meryl Carr Allen Collection; Don Mills.)

Four

FROM LIGHTHOUSE BUREAU TO COAST GUARD

LOWER DERRICK, LANDING COVE, EAST ANACAPA ISLAND, 1931. Since the 1853 wreck of the *Winfield Scott*, Anacapa Island was long considered a hazard to navigation. In 1909, Congress approved funds to build a light beacon atop East Anacapa. Island lessee H. Bay Webster chose the site for lighthouse inspectors and construction began in 1911. To access the top of the island, a landing derrick was constructed on the sheer cliff in Landing Cove. (CINP.)

THE FIRST LIGHT, EAST ANACAPA ISLAND, 1912. A 50-foot steel skeleton tower was constructed to hold the automated 530-candlepower acetylene light. Turned on in March 1912, the light flashed for one second, with a three second interval of darkness, followed by one second of light and ten seconds of darkness. The light was serviced every six months by the lighthouse tender *Sequoia* and remained in service until 1930. (CINP.)

LANDING COVE BEFORE THE STAIRS, EAST ANACAPA ISLAND, 1930. It took more than a year to complete relatively safe access from Landing Cove to the top of East Anacapa Island. Construction workers began at the bottom of the sheer cliff, blasted areas of the rock face, and worked their way to the top, constructing a multilevel landing with a hoist system. (CINP.)

LOWER DERRICK LANDING LOOKING NORTHEAST, EAST ANACAPA ISLAND, 1931. Access to the top of the mesa at East Anacapa Island was built into the rock face of a steep cliff several hundred feet high at Landing Cove. (CINP.)

Lower Derrick Landing, East Anacapa Island, 1931. During construction of the lower derrick landing, large rocks were removed from the cliff face using a clam shell. (CINP.)

CONSTRUCTION OF THE ISLAND'S ACCESS AT LANDING COVE, EAST ANACAPA ISLAND, 1931. The upper and lower boat landings at Landing Cove in East Anacapa Island were built into the cliff face just above the water line. (CINP.)

LADDERS TO ACCESS LANDING COVE DURING CONSTRUCTION, EAST ANACAPA ISLAND, 1931. Construction workers used ropes and long wooden ladders placed at various levels of the cliff face at Landing Cove to chisel areas for stairs and landings. (CINP.)

CONSTRUCTION OF THE UPPER DERRICK LANDING, EAST ANACAPA ISLAND, 1931. An area was leveled and prepared for construction of a retaining wall and cement slab near the top of the upper landing. (CINP.)

RETAINING WALL CONSTRUCTION AT UPPER DERRICK LANDING, EAST ANACAPA ISLAND, 1931. Concrete was poured for the retaining wall of the upper derrick landing in March 1931. Stairs embedded into the cliff face connected the lower derrick landing, 15 feet above mean water level, to the upper derrick landing, 250 feet above sea level. The lower derrick had a 40-foot, 5-ton-capacity boom, and the upper derrick had a 50-foot, 4-ton-capacity boom. (CINP.)

CONSTRUCTION OF THE ACCESS AT LANDING COVE, EAST ANACAPA ISLAND, 1933. By 1933, construction of the upper and lower derrick landings was completed. Because Landing Cove provides no safe anchorage, a hoist at the lower derrick was used to raise the Lighthouse Bureau's small vessel out of the water onto a dock platform. (CINP.)

MAINTENANCE OF THE ISLAND'S ACCESS AT LANDING COVE, EAST ANACAPA ISLAND, 1935. After completion of the access to the top of the mesa at Anacapa Island, men worked off loose rocks from the cliff face from a platform lowered from the upper derrick landing. (CINP.)

ROAD CONSTRUCTION LOOKING WEST, EAST ANACAPA ISLAND, 1930. Construction crews began their task of building a complex on the top of East Anacapa Island by excavating cuts into slopes; scraping off all vegetation, nests, and wildlife; and designing a dirt road system to connect all buildings. (CINP.)

FINISHED ROAD LOOKING NORTH, EAST ANACAPA ISLAND, 1931. By May 1931, the dirt roads had been scraped to the lighthouse location, the sites of the four lighthouse keepers' new residences, the water tank house, and other buildings. A 30,000-square-foot cement pad for rainwater collection was added to the revised phase-one contract awarded to Carpenter Brothers of Beverly Hills for $36,490. (CINP.)

ROTH CONSTRUCTION CAMP, EAST ANACAPA ISLAND, 1931. In 1928, the Bureau of Lighthouses allotted funds for construction of a major lighthouse complex, the last built on the California coast. Contracts were two-phased: landing facilities and roads, followed by buildings. Roth Construction of San Francisco won the first phase bid for $28,950, but defaulted soon after. Carpenter Brothers completed the landing derricks and roads. (CINP.)

CONSTRUCTION OF THE RAIN CATCHMENT, EAST ANACAPA ISLAND, 1931. Anacapa is a waterless island. In a time-consuming and labor-intensive effort, a one-sack cement mixer was used to mix the hundreds of yards of cement needed for the construction of an enormous concrete slab designed to catch rainwater, which was then stored in tanks. (CINP.)

GRADING FOR THE RAINSHED, EAST ANACAPA ISLAND, 1930. With the help of a small grader on tracks, a large area was cleared of all vegetation and leveled in preparation for cement to be poured over a 30,000-square-foot area. (CINP.)

CEMENT RAINSHED, EAST ANACAPA ISLAND, 1931. At 30,000 square feet, the cement catchment slab for the collection of rainwater covers more than half an acre. No longer used for its intended purpose, the slab serves as additional nesting ground for the prolific western gulls. (CINP.)

FIRST ASSISTANT KEEPER'S HOUSE, EAST ANACAPA ISLAND, 1931. M.W. Lippman of Los Angeles was awarded $74,595 for the second phase building contract, which included construction of a lighthouse powerhouse for the generator, oil house, and fog signal building. In addition, four lighthouse keepers' dwellings, a tank house, and a general service building were included in the plans. The design called for frame and stucco construction with terra cotta tile roofs in a Spanish-revival style. (CINP.)

REDWOOD WATER TANKS, EAST ANACAPA ISLAND, 1931. A large flat area was excavated and inset with platforms made of heavy wooden beams to accommodate two 55,000-gallon redwood water tanks. The beautifully crafted tanks of joined redwood were built by George Wendeler, who won the bid over three others. The tanks were protected from the sun by a large, white stucco church-like building. (CINP.)

WATER TANK HOUSE CONSTRUCTION, EAST ANACAPA ISLAND, 1931. East Anacapa is a dry island, and storage was needed for fresh water transported to the island by boat. Rainwater collected on the 30,000-square-foot rain shed was also stored in the two redwood tanks. The tanks were enclosed to protect the redwood from drying out and to keep birds and insects out of the open tops. (CINP.)

COMPLETED WATER TANK HOUSE, EAST ANACAPA ISLAND, 1931. The long-told tale about the Coast Guard enclosing the water tanks in a church-like building to keep them from being shot up by vandals is untrue, but still often repeated to this day. The tanks continue to hold water more than 87 years after their construction. (CINP.)

NEWLY COMPLETED COAST GUARD COMPLEX, EAST ANACAPA ISLAND, C. 1934. By the mid-1930s, when the various contractors had finished their work on Anacapa Island, in addition to the lighthouse and fog signal building, the island supported lower and upper deck landings at Landing Cove, four residences, a tank house, an oil house, and a general services building, all connected by a narrow roadway. (CINP.)

THE ISLAND'S ISOLATED "TOWN," EAST ANACAPA ISLAND. Eight men were stationed on East Anacapa Island. They rotated various duties so that everyone was qualified to work on the many phases of maintenance and operation of the station. One of these duties was giving a weather report every three hours by radio to the weather bureau in Los Angeles. (CINP.)

FROM LANDING COVE ON THE EAST TO THE RAINSHED ON THE WEST, EAST ANACAPA ISLAND.
The light station resembled a small town, with four residences along a main access road. Food, water, and other supplies were shipped from the mainland and hoisted up to the top of the island at Landing Cove. (CINP.)

LIGHTHOUSE TOWER FOUNDATION LAYOUT, EAST ANACAPA ISLAND, 1931. In August 1931, the new lighthouse tower foundation was placed at the site of the original 1912 light, 277 feet above sea level, the highest point on East Anacapa Island. It was built to support a three-story cylindrical concrete tower almost 50 feet tall, topped by a new third-order Fresnel lens. The fog signal building was built next to the lighthouse tower. (CINP.)

LIGHTHOUSE CONSTRUCTION, EAST ANACAPA ISLAND, 1931. Forms for the lower portion of the light tower were readied for the pouring of concrete by October. The lighthouse construction was completed in 1932, and the light was turned on for the first time on March 25, 1932. (CINP.)

LIGHTHOUSE AND FOG SIGNAL UNDER CONSTRUCTION, EAST ANACAPA ISLAND, 1931. The lighthouse was nearly completed by Christmas 1931, with 58 circular stairs leading up almost 40 feet to an eight-and-a-half-foot diameter lens housing. The light was activated on March 25, 1932, and contained a third-order Fresnel lens equipped with 114 glass prisms and a 2,000 watt, 1.2 million candlepower light that could be seen for 24 miles. (CINP.)

FOG SIGNAL BUILDING AND LIGHTHOUSE, EAST ANACAPA ISLAND. Next to the lighthouse is the diaphragm-type foghorn. It sounds a one- to two-second blast, followed by two seconds of silence. Then it sounds again for two seconds and completes its cycle with fourteen seconds of silence. (Photograph by Dan Harding.)

LIGHTHOUSE AND FOG SIGNAL BUILDING FACING THE MAINLAND, EAST ANACAPA ISLAND. The lighthouse visible from afar, atop East Anacapa Island, was built in the early 1930s and turned on for service on March 25, 1932. Anacapa Island was declared a national monument in 1938, and the following year, the Lighthouse Bureau went out of existence (1939). Management of the Anacapa Island lighthouse was transferred to the Coast Guard, along with all other light stations. (CINP.)

Five

FROM NATIONAL MONUMENT TO NATIONAL PARK

LIGHTHOUSE COMPLEX, EAST ANACAPA ISLAND, 1935. The Lighthouse Bureau's building complex was home to lighthouse keepers and their wives and families. In 1938, under President Roosevelt's Antiquities Act, both Anacapa and Santa Barbara Islands were declared a national monument. In 1939, the Lighthouse Bureau was dissolved, and the station was transferred to the Coast Guard. During World War II, the light was turned off (1942–1945). (CINP.)

Frenchy on West Anacapa Island, c. 1950. Fisherman Frenchy LeDreau continued living at his camp after the island became a national monument in 1938. During World War II, the Navy temporarily used Anacapa Island as a coastal lookout station. They removed Frenchy, only to have him repeatedly return. He stayed as a watchman, and there was always an ample supply of lobsters for the officers' mess. In return, Frenchy received surplus canned food. In the early 1950s, park service authorities, concerned over his advanced age, told him he had to leave the island. In 1954, in his 80th year, he regretfully agreed after suffering injuries in a fall. Frenchy died in Santa Barbara on April 21, 1962. He was 87. (CINP.)

FRENCHY'S CABIN, WEST ANACAPA ISLAND, C. 1948. In 1938, Channel Islands National Monument fell under the management of far-off Sequoia National Park. In 1957, headquarters were combined with Cabrillo National Monument in San Diego. After 30 years of neglect, an independent Channel Islands National Monument office was opened in Oxnard. Donald M. Robinson (1919–2004) served as the first superintendent from May 1967 to April 1974. (CINP.)

RANGER'S SEASONAL QUONSET HUT, WEST ANACAPA ISLAND, 1966. During the 1960s, the Navy transported a seasonal ranger who lived in a canvas Quonset hut part time at Frenchy's Cove during the summer. After 1967, with a local Channel Islands National Monument office in place in Oxnard, public curiosity about Anacapa Island began growing. (CINP.)

73

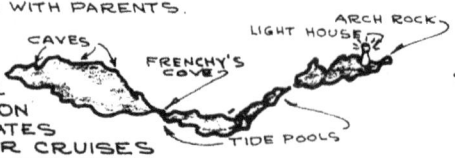
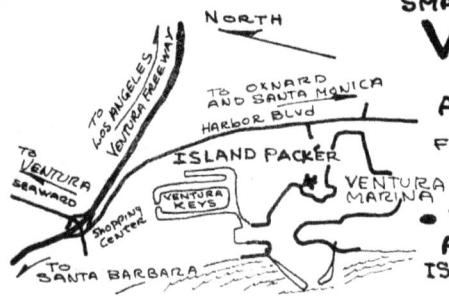

ISLAND PACKERS FIRST ADVERTISING FLYER, MAY 1968. A year after Channel Islands National Monument headquarters was moved to Oxnard (1967), Island Packers began offering trips to Frenchy's Cove, West Anacapa Island, charging $7.50 for a day trip with landing and $15 drop-off and pick-up for campers. For the first year of business, the Island Packers office was located in a 22-foot trailer at the Ventura Harbor launch ramp. A seasonal ranger was stationed at Frenchy's Cove on West Anacapa Island only in the summer months. (IPCO.)

BILL CONNALLY (1929–1987), FOUNDER OF ISLAND PACKERS. Bill Connally had always dreamed of starting a pack station in the High Sierra, but once the Channel Islands bug had bitten him, the thought of packing people into the islands occupied his grand scheming. In May 1968, with a freshly hauled out *Island Packer*, Bill Connally; his wife, Lil; and four children, Mark, Kirk, Brad, and Cherryl, began their business by taking tourists and campers to Frenchy's Cove on West Anacapa Island. (IPCO.)

ISLAND PACKER, FIRST VESSEL OWNED BY ISLAND PACKERS (1968–1969). Bill Connally purchased a 52-foot wood Liberty launch built for the US Navy in 1943. She had been converted to a charter fishing vessel in the 1950s and named *Verna F.* The vessel was licensed to carry 49 passengers with a crew of 3. With the *Island Packer,* Bill Connally's grand scheme of providing regularly scheduled transportation to Anacapa Island, a national monument since 1938, became reality. *Island Packer* was wrecked in a storm at Anacapa Island on December 8, 1969. The two people aboard were saved by the Coast Guard. (IPCO.)

CONNALLY FAMILY CHRISTENING *ISLAND PACKER,* 1968. After an extensive makeover and renaming, the *Island Packer* was launched at Anchors Way, Ventura Harbor, on May 12, 1968. It was said that, "What the vessel lacked in amenities, the crew made up in enthusiasm!" There were four gold stars following the name—one for each of the Connally children. From left to right are Cherryl, Brad, Kirk (kneeling), Mark, and parents Bill and Lil Connally. (IPCO.)

PAISANO, SECOND VESSEL OWNED BY ISLAND PACKERS (1969–1975). In 1969, Island Packers leased and then bought *Paisano*—a 63-foot wood hulled US Navy vessel modified as a sport fishing boat with 26 bunks and a galley. As the business grew, additional boats were leased by Island Packers, and island trips were expanded to include Santa Barbara Island, also a national monument, and privately owned Santa Cruz Island. In 1975, condemned by the Coast Guard for dry rot issues, *Paisano* was removed from service. (IPCO.)

ISLAND PACKERS ORANGE SKIFF OPERATIONS. Mark Connally is pictured standing at center. From the beginning of Island Packers in 1968, through the next three decades, all Anacapa Island passengers were transported to shore by skiff. For the first year, passengers were rowed ashore by one of the Connally boys, Mark, Kirk, or Brad. Outboards were added when they got the *Paisano*. (IPCO.)

WILLIAM EHORN, SUPERINTENDENT. Bill Ehorn was superintendent of Channel Islands National Monument from 1974 to 1980. He was instrumental in arranging for San Miguel Island to be opened to the public through an agreement with the Navy, four years before Channel Islands National Park was created. He assisted Congressman Robert J. Lagomarsino in drafting the park legislation, and became the park's first superintendent (1980–1989). Ehorn was a charismatic and beloved superintendent, held in high regard by the private island owners. (Bill Ehorn.)

CHANNEL ISLANDS NATIONAL PARK STAFF, 1981. Pictured from left to right are (first row) Dana Seagers, Roger LeMere, Anne Bellamy, Diane Morrison, Heather Leone, Norma Betta, Nicholas Whelan, Kern Jettmar, and James Bellamy; (second row) Bill Ehorn, Kermit Bessett, Michael Hill, Christina Horton, Craig Johnson, George Leone, Gary Robertson, David Stoltz, and Wayne Pero. Bill Ehorn served until 1989, when he transferred to Redwoods National Park until his retirement in 1995. (Bill Ehorn.)

WE SEVEN, THIRD VESSEL OWNED BY ISLAND PACKERS. In 1969, the 40-foot wood-hulled dive boat We Seven was the third vessel purchased by Island Packers. She was built by Jeffries Boats in Venice, California, and licensed to carry 29 with a crew of 3. We Seven was ultimately sold to a sport fishing business in 1985. (IPCO.)

ORANGE SKIFF OPERATION AT LANDING COVE, WEST ANACAPA ISLAND. For the first 33 years in business, Island Packers towed custom-designed wooden orange skiffs across the channel behind their boats and used them to land passengers at Anacapa Island. At East Anacapa, passengers were skiffed from the boat to the vertical ladder at Landing Cove. Today, their catamarans can power up to the ladder without skiffs being used. (IPCO.)

SUNFISH, FOURTH VESSEL OWNED BY ISLAND PACKERS. Kirk Connally purchased *Sunfish* for his family's business in 1978. *Sunfish*, a 55-foot sport-fishing vessel, was built in 1960 by Jeffries Boats in Venice. Two years after *Sunfish* entered the Island Packers fleet, the family business became the official concessionaire to the newly created Channel Islands National Park, established in 1980. *Sunfish* served as the company's primary vessel for more than two decades. (IPCO.)

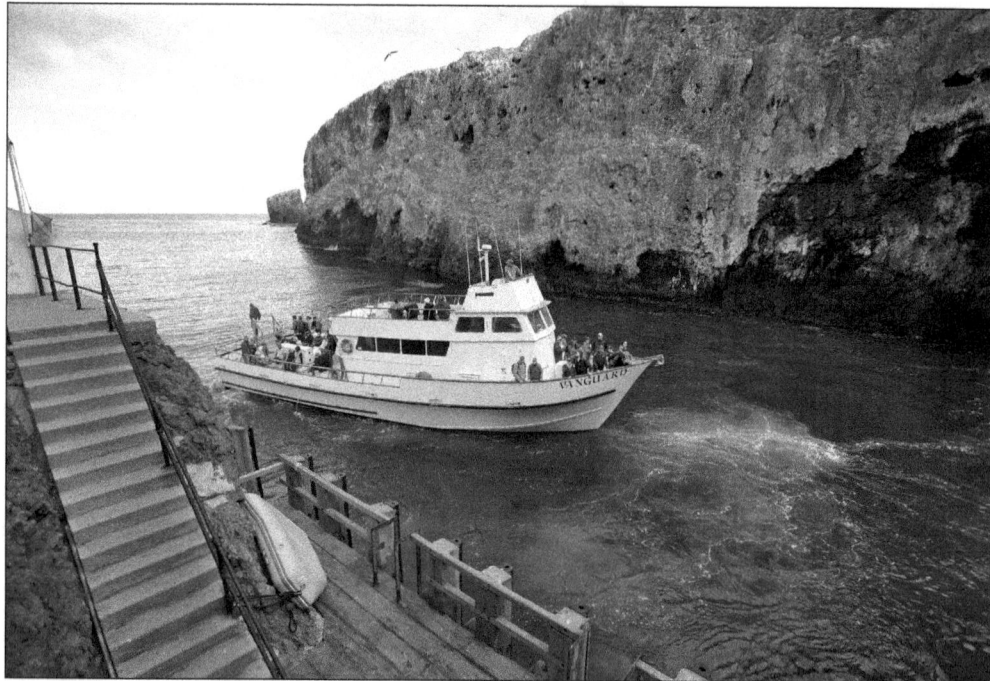

VANGUARD, ISLAND PACKERS ANACAPA ISLAND FLEET VESSEL. *Vanguard*, built in 1991, is used exclusively for trips to Anacapa Island. She generally runs out of Channel Islands Harbor from an Island Packers office annex. At 65 feet long, *Vanguard* is licensed to carry 89 passengers and 3 crew members. (Photograph by Doug Magnum.)

ISLANDER LEAVING VENTURA HARBOR, 2001. In 2001, Island Packers acquired *Islander*, first of the company's three New Zealand-designed high-speed aluminum catamarans. These vessels are built by All American Marine in Bellingham, Washington. They are 65 feet long and licensed for 149 passengers and 4 crew members. The catamarans carry inflatable skiffs onboard, thus wooden skiffs are no longer towed across the channel. (Photograph by Flash Wheeler; IPCO.)

ISLAND ADVENTURE, 2013. On May 12, 2018, Island Packers celebrated its 50th anniversary of safely transporting more than a million passengers—day-trippers and campers—to Anacapa Island. The Connally family began business when Anacapa Island was a national monument, operating for 12 years before the park was established. In 1980, when Channel Islands National Park was created, Island Packers became the official concessionaire. (Photograph by Kevin L. Bailey.)

FOOTPATH APPROACH ACROSS EAST ANACAPA ISLAND. In 1962, the Coast Guard began converting Anacapa to an unattended operation. In 1967, three of the beautiful houses were demolished before the superintendent of Channel Islands National Monument, Don Robinson (1919–2004), gave notice that the Park Service was interested in the buildings. In 1970, the Park Service assumed responsibility of the remaining buildings, and in 1980, Anacapa Island became part of Channel Islands National Park. (Photograph by Dan Harding.)

RANGER'S RESIDENCE, EAST ANACAPA ISLAND. The first assistant lighthouse keeper's house was one of four Mission Revival–style houses built by the Lighthouse Bureau in 1931. The three other houses were demolished by the Coast Guard in 1967. In 2009, the Coast Guard property on East Anacapa Island was transferred to the park service. This remaining historic house serves as the Anacapa Island ranger's residence. (Photograph by Dan Harding.)

FACING WEST ON EAST ANACAPA ISLAND. There are two miles of trails on top of East Anacapa Island that meander to dramatic overlooks and magnificent coastal views. Hikers must stay on the trails, away from the island's sharp cliffs, for safety and to protect fragile vegetation and nesting seabirds. No off-trail hiking is allowed. (Photograph by Dan Harding.)

PRIMITIVE CAMPGROUND, EAST ANACAPA ISLAND, 1986. There are seven campsites on East Anacapa Island available to the public by advance reservation, and camping is permitted for up to two weeks. Campsites hold four to six people. Picnic table, food storage box, and public pit toilet are provided. There is no fresh water available and no electricity. All personal supplies, food, and gear must be transported by the camper. If something is forgotten, one goes without. (Photograph by Marla Daily; SCIF.)

LIGHTHOUSE, EAST ANACAPA ISLAND. The Anacapa Island Lighthouse was built in the early 1930s by the Bureau of Lighthouses and turned on on March 25, 1932. Seven years later, the Bureau of Lighthouses was abolished and lighthouse functions were turned over to the Coast Guard, where responsibility remains today. From the 1930s through the 1960s, a series of lighthouse keepers were assigned to Anacapa Island until operations became automated and the lighthouse became unattended. (Photograph by Dan Harding.)

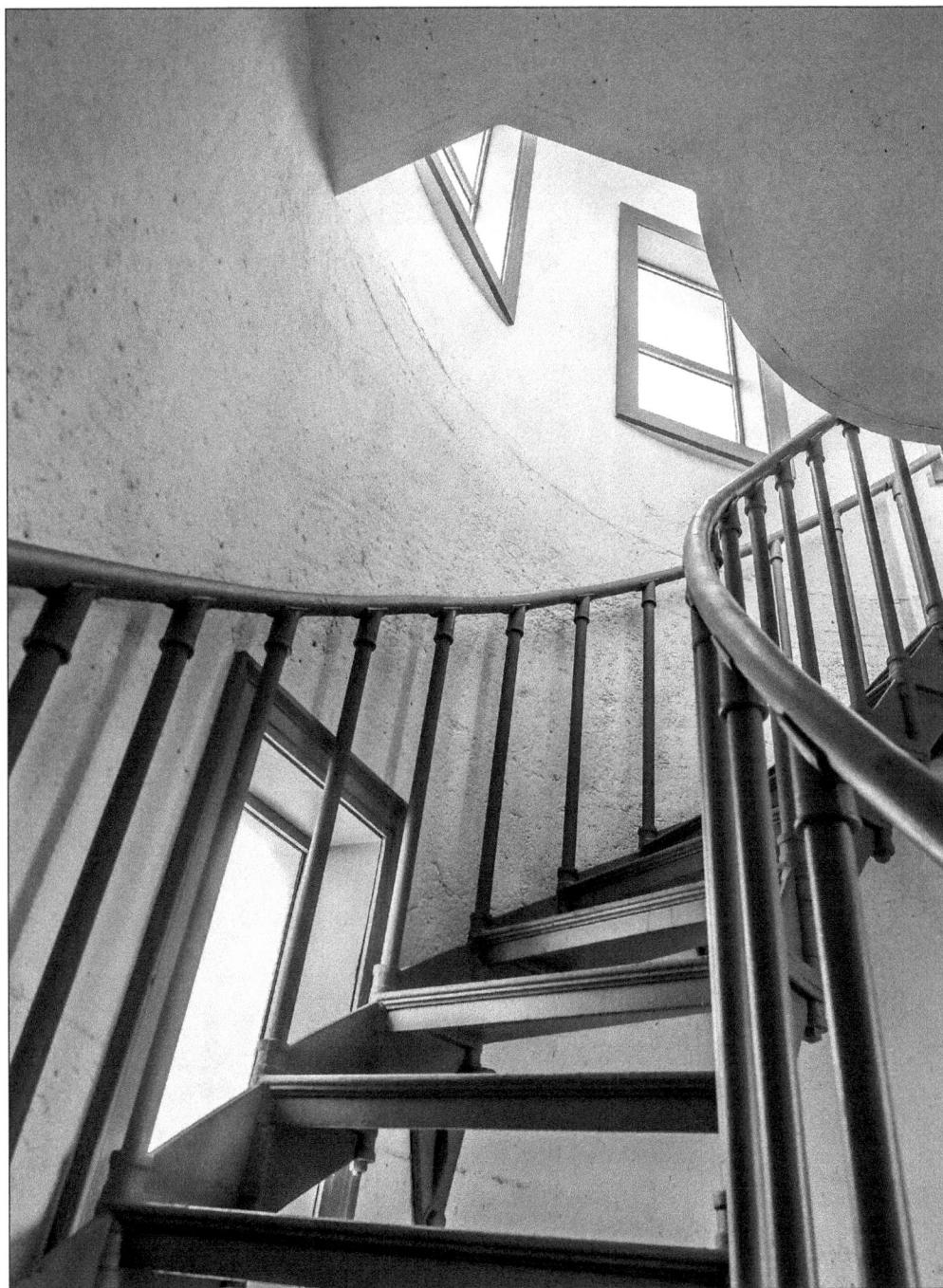

LIGHTHOUSE INTERIOR, EAST ANACAPA ISLAND. An iron spiral staircase leads from ground level up the interior wall of the lighthouse tower to a height of almost 50 feet. The Anacapa Island Lighthouse is the last one established on the California coast. (Photograph by Dan Harding.)

LIGHTHOUSE REPLACEMENT LENS, EAST ANACAPA ISLAND. The Coast Guard continues to maintain the Anacapa Island aids to navigation. It removed the original third-order Fresnel lens in 1990 and replaced it with a plastic lens. The original lens is on display in the park service visitor center on East Anacapa Island, formerly the Coast Guard's general services building. (Photograph by Dan Harding.)

Six

WILDLIFE ON AND AROUND ANACAPA ISLAND

EUROPEAN RABBIT (ORYCTOLAGUS CUNICULUS). This museum specimen was collected on East Anacapa Island by Jack Von Bloeker in 1940. Anacapa, a waterless island, has a total of only four native terrestrial vertebrate species: one mammal, the endemic island deer mouse; one amphibian, the Channel Islands slender salamander; and two reptiles, the western side-blotched lizard and southern alligator lizard. Introduced populations of sheep were removed by about 1938; feral rabbits in the mid-1960s; and black rats in 2001–2002. Cats and dogs, once kept by island residents, are no longer allowed on the island. (LACM.)

ANACAPA ISLAND DEER MOUSE (*PEROMYSCUS MANICULATUS ANACAPAE*). The deer mouse is the only native terrestrial mammal on Anacapa Island. Deer mice are common to all eight California Channel Islands, and each island has developed its own distinct subspecies. Mice are curious and prolific on all three Anacapa islets. Although the mice are primarily nocturnal, they may be seen at any time, scurrying around all island habitats. Campers must take care to keep food in mouse-proof containers. Mice can be expected to inspect tents and camping gear. (Photograph by Holly Gellerman.)

CHANNEL ISLANDS SLENDER SALAMANDER (*BATRACHOSEPS PACIFICUS*). This is the only amphibian found on Anacapa Island. This island endemic form is also found on Santa Cruz, Santa Rosa, and San Miguel Islands. Because their legs are so small, they have a wormlike appearance. These lungless salamanders breathe through their skin, which requires them to live in damp environments on land. They move about on the ground only during times of high humidity or rain. (CINP.)

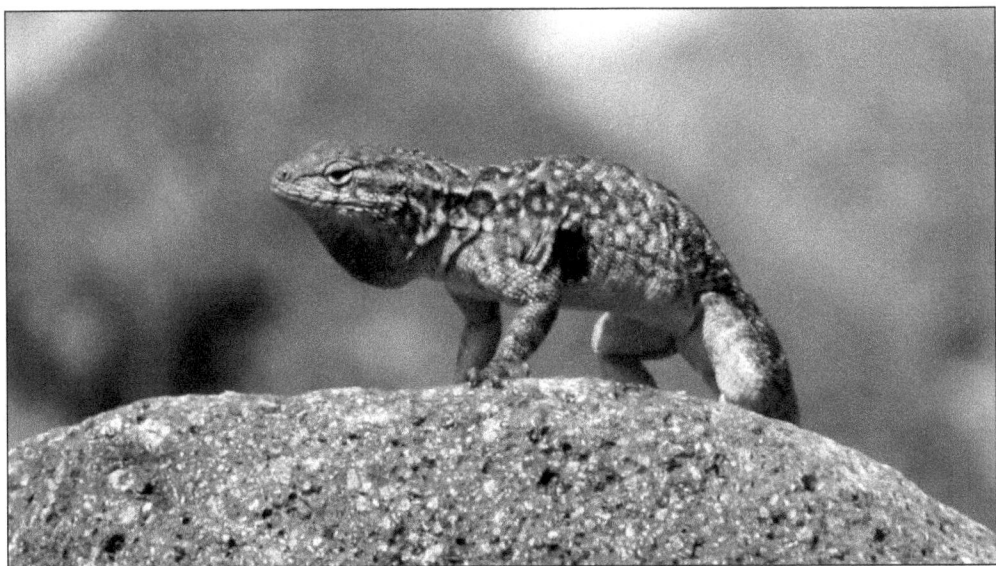

WESTERN SIDE-BLOTCHED LIZARD (*UTA STANSBURIANA*). One of two reptile species found on Anacapa Island, this endemic form is also found on Santa Cruz, Santa Catalina, and San Clemente Islands. These lizards are monogamous and only live about one year. Males are often seen doing push-ups to defend their territory. They eat a wide variety of insects and arthropods, including scorpions, spiders, mites, ticks, and sowbugs. Some vegetable material is also eaten, possibly for water. (Photograph by Tim Hauf.)

SOUTHERN ALLIGATOR LIZARD (*ELEGARIA MULTICARINATA*). This species of reptile is commonly found on Anacapa, San Miguel, Santa Rosa, and Santa Cruz Islands in Channel Islands National Park. Just like snakes, alligator lizards shed their skin in a single intact piece by essentially turning it inside out as they crawl out of it. They are large lizards that can grow up to one foot in length. Alligator lizards live up to 15 years. (Photograph by David Feliz.)

BLACK RATS (RATTUS RATTUS) ON ANACAPA ISLAND. Black rats are thought to be native to India, but through global human travel they have been introduced to all continents. Rats may have arrived on Anacapa Island as early as the 1853 wreck of the *Winfield Scott*. Channel Islands National Park began a rat-poisoning program in 2001, dropping poison pellets by helicopter. Just over two years and $3 million later, rats were exterminated. Anacapa Island was declared rat-free in 2003. (CINP.)

ANACAPA ISLAND TIDE POOL.
Anacapa Island tide pools
are some of the richest
and most diverse found
within southern California.
Anemones, sea stars, urchins,
limpets, periwinkles, chitons,
barnacles, mussels, and many
other beautiful species can
be seen at numerous pristine
tide pool sites. The south
side of West Anacapa Island
behind Frenchy's Cove has
particularly spectacular beds
of tide pools. (Photograph
by Dan Harding.)

SEA STARS DINING ON A MUSSEL-COVERED INTERTIDAL ROCK. Marine scientists have undertaken the difficult task of replacing the starfish's common name with sea star because the starfish is not a fish. It is an echinoderm, closely related to sea urchins and sand dollars. There are some 1,800 species of sea stars living in all the world's oceans. Although the five-arm varieties are the most common, species with 10, 20, and even 40 arms exist. Some species can live up to 35 years. (Photograph by Steve Munch.)

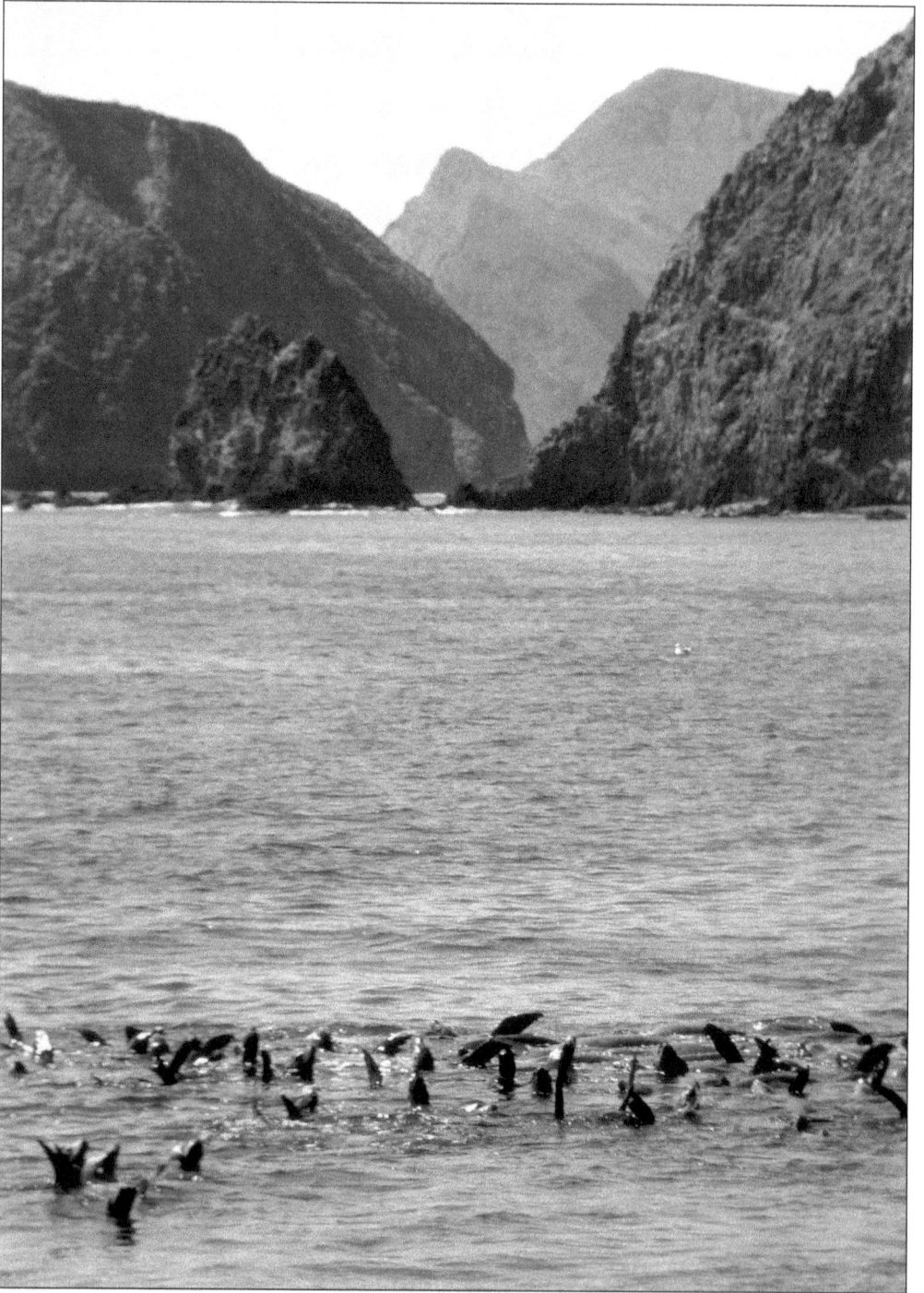

RAFT OF SEA LIONS, EAST ANACAPA ISLAND. California sea lions are often found resting on the ocean's surface with their flippers out of the water. By exposing their poorly insulated flippers to the warmth of the sun, sea lions can regulate their body temperature in a process called thermoregulation. Sun-warmed flippers transfer warmed blood throughout the animal's body. (Photograph by Marla Daily; SCIF.)

CALIFORNIA SEA LION (*ZALOPHUS CALIFORNIANUS*). California sea lions rest and breed on Anacapa Island. They are often seen hauled-out on offshore rocks, and are frequently encountered by snorkelers and divers in the kelp forest. Two overlooks atop East Anacapa's steep cliffs at Cathedral Cove and Pinniped Point provide excellent spots to look down on seals and sea lions along the island's rocky shores. (Photograph by Steve Munch.)

CALIFORNIA SEA LION AND CALIFORNIA BROWN PELICANS, EAST ANACAPA ISLAND. Anacapa Island is covered with a variety of wildlife. Seabirds and pinnipeds coexist on Anacapa Island, often competing for the same space and the same fish food. (Photograph by Dan Harding.)

HARBOR SEALS ON ANACAPA ISLAND (*PHOCA VITULINA*). Harbor seals rest and breed on Anacapa Island. They can often be spotted on rocks near the water's edge with their head and flippers elevated and being warmed by the sun. Unlike other pinnipeds, there is little difference in size between males and females, each reaching five to six feet in length. (Photograph by Dan Harding.)

HARBOR SEAL PUP ON ANACAPA ISLAND. Harbor seals can easily be distinguished from sea lions because they lack external ears. When they move, they drag their hind flippers behind, unlike sea lions that use their hind flippers for walking. Harbor seals can live for about 40 years. (Photograph by Dan Harding.)

A POD OF COMMON DOLPHINS OFFSHORE FROM ANACAPA ISLAND. The waters surrounding Anacapa Island are home to many diverse species of dolphins and porpoises. Common dolphin are divided into two species, short-beaked and long-beaked, both of which occur locally. In addition, Pacific white-sided dolphins, bottlenose dolphins, Risso's dolphins, and Dall's porpoise are all channel residents. (Photograph by Donna Mitnick.)

COMMON DOLPHIN (DELPHINUS). Both short-beaked and long-beaked dolphin species range from about six to eight feet in length, with males generally being longer and heavier. They have dark backs with light-colored sides and bellies. Common dolphins often travel in aggregations of hundreds or even thousands of dolphins. They do not fare well in captivity. (Photograph by Richard Jackson.)

BOTTLENOSE DOLPHIN (*TURSIOPS TRUNCATUS*). This dolphin species is the most well-known of all dolphins, likely because of its frequent appearances on television and in film, and its popularity with the captivity industry. They grow to 13 feet in length and often ride bow waves of vessels. Bottlenose dolphins sometimes show curiosity toward humans in or near water. They can live for more than 40 years. (Photograph by Tim Hauf.)

PACIFIC WHITE-SIDED DOLPHIN (*LAGENORHYNCHUS OBLIQUIDENS*). These dolphins keep close company and swim in groups of 10 to 100 or more. They can often be seen bow-riding and doing somersaults. Members form a close-knit group and will often care for a sick or injured dolphin. Young dolphins communicate with a touch of a flipper as they swim beside adults. (Photograph by Giancarlo Thomae.)

RISSO'S DOLPHIN (*GRAMPUS GRISEUS*). These blunt-headed dolphins typically can be seen in the Santa Barbara Channel in groups of a few animals to perhaps 30 individuals. They bear lots of scars, made by the teeth of their own kind or by the beaks of their preferred prey: squid. Grampus, as they are often called, are one of the largest species of dolphins. They dwell over deepwater in order to hunt migrating squid. (Photograph by Giancarlo Thomae.)

KILLER WHALE (*ORCINUS ORCA*) OFF EAST ANACAPA ISLAND. In addition to dolphins and porpoises, the waters surrounding Anacapa Island are home to many diverse species of whales. Toothed whale species in the channel include pilot whales, killer whales, and occasionally, sperm whales. Orca often dine on seals and sea lions. (Photograph by Steve Munch.)

GRAY WHALE (*ESCHRICHTIUS ROBUSTUS*). Gray whales migrate 10,000 miles each year, from feeding grounds in the Bering Sea to calving lagoons in Baja California and back. They transit the Santa Barbara Channel in the winter headed south and again in the spring headed north. Females are often sighted on their return journey north with a newborn at their side. (Photograph by Richard Jackson.)

HUMPBACK WHALE (*MEGAPTERA NOVAEANGLIAE*). Baleen whale species sighted in the channel include humpback, gray, finback, minke, and the largest of all whale species, the blue whale. Generally, humpback whales can be seen in the Santa Barbara Channel from mid-May to mid-September. They are often seen breeching out of the water, performing aerobatic leaps. (Photograph by Richard Jackson.)

BLUE WHALE (*BALAENOPTERA MUSCULUS*) SOUNDING OFF EAST ANACAPA ISLAND. Blue whales are part-time residents of the waters off the California Channel Islands. They range from about 80 to 100 feet in length and are the largest animal on earth. Blue whales live in all oceans of the world. They can be seen off the Channel Islands from about February through July, with peak numbers occurring in April. (Photograph by Jeanette Tonnies.)

AERIAL VIEW OF A BLUE WHALE (*BALAENOPTERA MUSCULUS*). Blue whales are filter feeders. Instead of teeth, they have 300 to 400 fringed baleen plates that hang from their upper jaws and strain their food. They eat krill, a small shrimplike invertebrate found in colder waters. (NOAA.)

SPOUTING BLUE WHALE (*BALAENOPTERA MUSCULUS*). Blue whales have a general cruising speed of 5 miles per hour but can accelerate up to 20 miles per hour when needed. Surprisingly, they are the loudest animals on the planet. Their sounds can reach 188 decibels. (Photograph by Richard Jackson.)

Seven

BIRDS, RESIDENT AND OTHERWISE

SEABIRDS ABOVE LANDING COVE, EAST ANACAPA ISLAND. Thousands of birds use Anacapa Island as a nesting area due to the relative lack of disturbance and predators. Nine species of seabirds nest on Anacapa Island: ashy storm-petrels; double-crested, Brandt's, and pelagic cormorants; California brown pelicans; western gulls; pigeon guillemots; Scripp's murrelets; and Cassin's auklets. (Photograph by Dan Harding.)

WESTERN GULL (*LARUS OCCIDENTALIS*) WITH CHICKS, EAST ANACAPA ISLAND. Western gulls are the most conspicuous birds on Anacapa Island. Based on a bird tagged in 1973 and re-sighted in 2007, they are known to live up to 34 years. (Photograph by Dan Harding.)

WESTERN GULL DIVING ON A VISITOR, EAST ANACAPA ISLAND. During nesting season, western gulls, screaming and crying out, are known to dive on intruders. Like most gulls, they are opportunistic feeders, capturing live prey, scavenging refuse, and stealing food from other gulls and even seals and sea lions. (Photograph by Dan Harding.)

WESTERN GULLS AT INSPIRATION POINT, EAST ANACAPA ISLAND. Anacapa Island is host to one of the largest colonies of western gulls in the world. They are clever and curious, and will steal food left exposed in daypacks and at campsites. (Photograph by Dan Harding.)

DOUBLE-CRESTED CORMORANT (*PHALACROCORAX AURITUS*), ANACAPA ISLAND. Three species of cormorants nest on Anacapa Island: double-crested, Brandt's, and pelagic. Cormorants are large waterbirds with small heads and kinked necks. They dive to catch fish and spread their wings to dry in the sun. (Photograph by Tom Haglund.)

CORMORANTS AND WESTERN GULLS AT ARCH ROCK, EAST ANACAPA ISLAND. In 1855, W.M. Johnson of the Coast Survey noted, "The east end of [Anacapa] is a place of resort of countless numbers of sea-birds, which deposit their eggs and bring up their young in perfect security from the disturbance of man. I doubt very much whether previous to our mission that part of the island had ever been visited by a white man." (Photograph by Dan Harding.)

PELAGIC CORMORANT (*PHALACROCORAX PELAGICUS*), ANACAPA ISLAND. Also sometimes referred to as a shag, the pelagic cormorant is the smallest of the three cormorant species that nest on Anacapa Island. Like the other cormorant species, they hold out their wings to dry. (Photograph by David Pereksta; BOEM.)

PIGEON GUILLEMOT (*CEPPHUS COLUMBA*), ANACAPA ISLAND. These seabirds are summer nesters on Anacapa Island, where they usually lay their eggs in rocky crevices and cavities along cliffs. Both parents incubate a single egg, and successful chicks usually return to their natal colony to breed. Pigeon guillemots dive into the water to feed on fish and invertebrates. They can be found either in small colonies or in isolated pairs. (Photograph by David Pereksta; BOEM.)

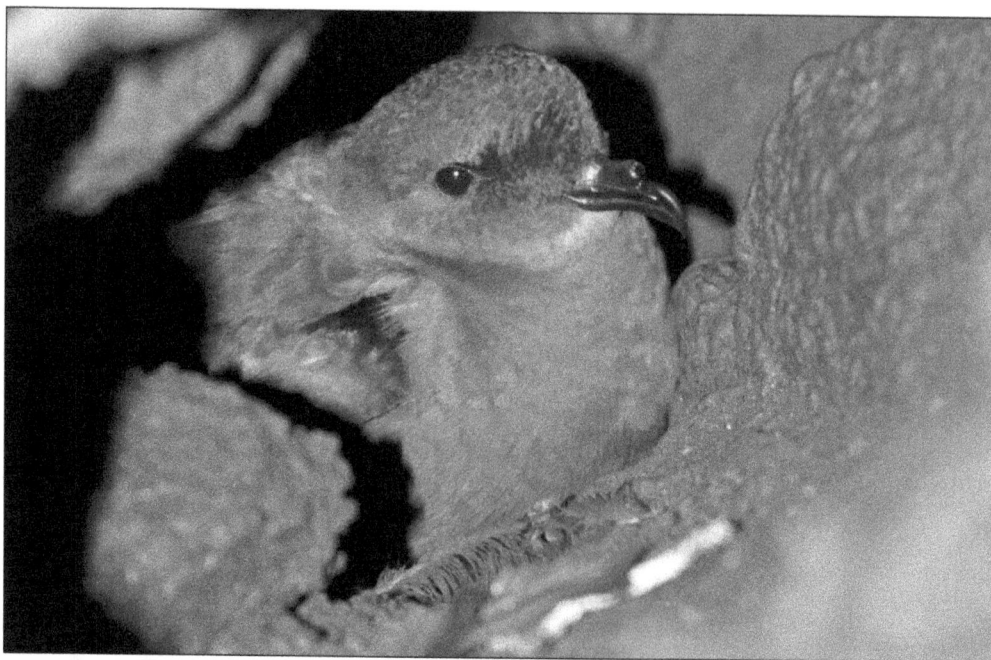

ASHY STORM PETREL (*OCEANODROMA HOMOCHROA*), ANACAPA ISLAND. The ashy storm petrel is a scarce seabird common only within its range off California and northwestern Baja California, Mexico. The species relies upon the isolated breeding grounds of several Channel Islands, where it nests in rock crevices along cliffs, offshore rocks, and under driftwood in sea caves. (Photograph by David Pereksta; BOEM.)

SCRIPP'S MURRELET (*SYNTHLIBORAMPHUS SCRIPPSI*), ANACAPA ISLAND. This is among the world's rarest seabirds, and 80 percent of their population is found on the California Channel Islands. They too nest in rock crevices along steep edges around the periphery of islands, including Anacapa. (Photograph by David Pereksta; BOEM.)

CALIFORNIA BROWN PELICAN (*PELECANUS OCCIDENTALIS CALIFORNICUS*), ANACAPA ISLAND. The only nesting populations of California brown pelicans along the west coast of North America are found at the California Channel Islands, where they are resident on all five park islands. They are strong swimmers and live to 40 years in the wild. West Anacapa Island is home to the largest breeding colony of California brown pelicans. (Photograph by Richard Jackson.)

BALD EAGLE SHOT ON ANACAPA ISLAND IN 1892. Isaac Proctor Browne (1871–1957), a Santa Paula grocer, shot this bald eagle on Anacapa Island when he was 21 years old. In 1934, the mounted specimen was donated to the Museum of Ventura County by Leroy S. "Roy" Beckley (1858–1939). How he acquired it is unknown. This is the only preserved bald eagle specimen from Anacapa Island, although at least 30 eagle eggs from Anacapa Island nests are in museum collections. (SCIF.)

RED-TAILED HAWK (*BUTEO JAMAICENSIS*). Anacapa Island is home to several species of raptors, including the bald eagle, red-tailed hawk, barn owl, American kestrel, and peregrine falcon. Red-tailed hawks are uncommon residents, usually with 10 records or less per season. (Photograph by Tom Haglund.)

AMERICAN KESTREL (*FALCO SPARVERIUS*), ANACAPA ISLAND. Kestrels are North America's smallest falcon. They are also one of the most colorful of all raptors. Kestrels are fairly common residents of Anacapa Island, present in small numbers. (Photograph by Tom Haglund.)

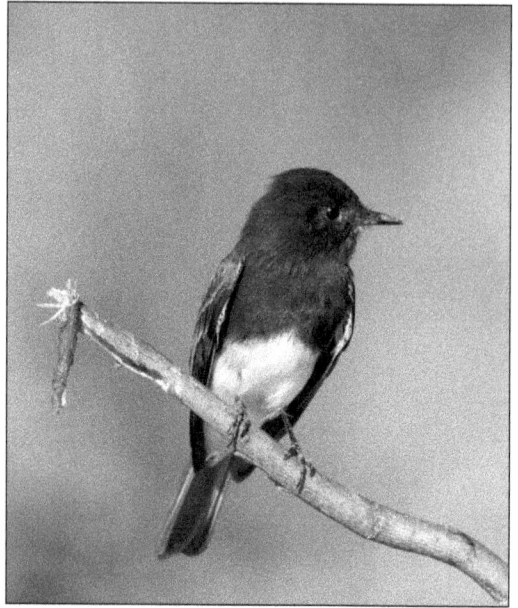

LANDBIRDS ON ANACAPA ISLAND. Clockwise from upper left, pictured here are the American oystercatcher, black phoebe, house finch, and western meadowlark. There are about two dozen species of land birds that nest on Anacapa Island: bald eagle, red-tailed hawk, American kestrel, peregrine falcon, American oystercatcher, black oystercatcher, mourning dove, barn owl, white-throated swift, black phoebe, Hutton's vireo, common raven, barn swallow, rock wren, European starling, chipping sparrow, western meadowlark, and house finch. Of these, six are endemic subspecies found on one or more islands and nowhere else: Allen's hummingbird, Pacific slope flycatcher, Bewick's wren, orange-crowned warbler, rufous-crowned sparrow, and song sparrow. Landbird populations and species compositions change from year to year, depending on mainland species that reach the islands, changes in habitats, competitors or predators that arrive or leave the islands, or disturbance. (Photographs by Tom Haglund.)

Eight

PLANTS, NATIVE AND INTRODUCED

CHOLLA (OPUNTIA PROLIFERA), EAST ANACAPA ISLAND, 1946. Anacapa Island supports about 265 species of plants, including 190 native taxa and 75 non-native species. Of these, two species are found only on Anacapa Island, and at least 22 are restricted to two or more of the California Channel Islands. (Photograph by Phil Orr; SBBG.)

LORENZO GORDIN YATES (1837–1909). In 1893, Lorenzo Yates was among the first to collect plants on all four northern Channel Islands, including Anacapa. A dentist by trade, he had moved to Santa Barbara in 1881, where he became a founder of the Santa Barbara Society of Natural History. Yates was a naturalist, investigator, collector, and a specialist in ferns, general botany, conchology, mineralogy, paleontology, and North American Indians. In 1890, he described his namesake Yates Cave on West Anacapa Island. (SMHM.)

HISTORIC EUCALYPTUS TREES ON MIDDLE ANACAPA ISLAND. A small grove of eucalyptus trees marks the site of former ranch buildings on Middle Anacapa Island. The trees were planted in the 1880s during the years Ezekiel Elliott (1833–1912) and his son Joseph Vincent Elliott (1860–1943) ran sheep on the island (1882–1897). (Photograph by Marla Daily; SCIF.)

COREOPSIS (COREOPSIS GIGANTEA) IN BLOOM ON EAST ANACAPA ISLAND. From March through May, blooming Coreopsis dominates the landscape with showy yellow flowers bursting forth from stout succulent stems growing from a main stalk several feet tall. Western gulls compete for space on Coreopsis, often breaking the plants. (SBBG.)

SPRING COREOPSIS BLOOM, EAST ANACAPA ISLAND. The Coreopsis plants provide shelter and perches for seabirds and land birds, as well as nesting habitat. Their prolific seeds provide abundant food for the endemic Anacapa deer mouse and many small birds. (Photograph by Dan Harding.)

ISLAND TREE MALLOW (*LAVATERS ASSURGENTIFLORA*). The island tree mallow is native only to the California Channel Islands. Plants often grow to a height of six feet or more. On East Anacapa Island, however, Mallow are often battered and broken by a preponderance of western gulls. The plant's showy, slightly striped pink flowers attract butterflies. (Photograph by Steve Junak; SBBG.)

NORTHERN ISLAND MORNING GLORY (*CALYSTEGIA MACROSTEGIA S. MACROSTEGIA*). This native perennial vine, with its pinkish-white funnelform flowers, is found in bloom from April through July. It is often found climbing over and around other plants, hence its other common name: island false bindweed. (Photograph by Steve Junak; SBBG.)

JUNAK'S DESERT DANDELION (*MALACOTHRIX JUNAKII*). Named for botanist Steve Junak, this rare annual herb is one of two plants endemic to Anacapa Island. It was described to science as a new species in 1997 and is known from just two occurrences. (Photograph by Steve Junak; SBBG.)

SPRING VIEW TO THE WEST, EAST ANACAPA ISLAND. Walking East Anacapa Island's two-mile trail system allows visitors to see both native and introduced vegetation. Although for much of the year the island looks brown and lifeless and trampled by western gulls, when winter rains come, the landscape is transformed. (Photograph by Marla Daily; SCIF.)

SEASIDE DAISY (*ERIGERON GLAUCUS*). This perennial daisy is native to California and Oregon, where it is found along mainland and island coastlines. Showy flowers have yellow centers with petals of deep blue and purple to nearly white. (Photograph by Steve Junak; SBBG.)

SAND LETTUCE (*DUDLEYA CAESPITOSA*). This species of *Dudleya* is endemic to California, where it grows along the coastline in the southern half of the state. Its frosty grey-white rosettes and long-lasting, orange-yellow flowers attract hummingbirds. The plants bloom throughout the spring and summer months. (Photograph by Steve Junak; SBBG.)

CRYSTALLINE ICE PLANT (*MESEMBRYANTHEMUM CRYSTALLINUM*) ON EAST ANACAPA ISLAND. crystalline ice plant is an invasive plant on East Anacapa Island, where is has been displacing native species, including *Coreopsis* and *Dudleya*. Tiny beads along the plant's stems are swollen with water. They crush open when trod upon. The species is part of an invasive plant removal program on Anacapa Island. (Photograph by Dan Harding.)

ICE PLANT (*MALEPHORA CROCEA*). Red ice plant is native to Africa and is often grown as an ornamental groundcover. It was introduced to Anacapa Island by Coast Guard personnel in the 1940s and 1950s for landscaping and erosion control. The ice plant spread rapidly, blanketing large areas and negatively affecting the island's native ecosystem of plants and animals. Channel Islands National Park has implemented a restoration project to remove the ice plant. (Photograph by Steve Junak; SBBG.)

YARROW (*ACHILLEA MILLEFOLIUM*). Yarrow, a member of the sunflower family, is a perennial herb that is native to California and found on all five islands in Channel Islands National Park. Its tiny ray flowers, varying in shades of white to pink, bloom in clusters along feathery-leaved erect stems. (SBBG.)

ORB-WEAVER SPIDER ON ANACAPA ISLAND. Vegetation on Anacapa Island supports a great assemblage of insect fauna, including orb-weavers, the most common group of spiders that build spiral wheel-shaped webs. They are non-aggressive, and their webs are often found spanning plants along the trails. (Photograph by Steve Junak; SBBG.)

Nine

WATER SPORTS AND THE 12.2-MILE SWIM

WATERWORLD AT ARCH ROCK, EAST ANACAPA ISLAND. Offshore, giant bladder kelp grows in dense stands forming underwater kelp forests. Over 1,000 species of marine plants and animals can be found within the Channel Islands' kelp forests. Giant bladder kelp grows in individual stipes often up to 150 feet long. Each unbranched stipe is lined with blades, each with a gas bladder at its base. Collectively, the gas bladders hold the algae upright in the water column. (Photograph by Dan Harding.)

ABOVE AND BELOW WATER, EAST ANACAPA ISLAND. The world of Anacapa Island may be explored in multiple ways both on shore and off: hiking, camping, kayaking, snorkeling, or scuba diving. The Channel Islands National Park boundary extends 1.8 km (1 nautical mile) from the shore. The Channel Islands National Marine Sanctuary boundary extends 10.8 km (6 nautical miles) from shore. (Photograph by Dan Harding.)

PADDLE-WHEEL SHAFT OF THE *WINFIELD SCOTT*. On December 2, 1853, the 225-foot wooden steam-powered paddle-wheeler *Winfield Scott* (1850–1853) collided with Middle Anacapa Island in a heavy fog. The wreck lies offshore on the north side of Middle Anacapa Island. The site is listed in the National Register of Historic Places. (Photograph by Robert Schwemmer; NOAA.)

GRUMMAN AVENGER OFF ANACAPA ISLAND. During World War II, a Grumman Avenger torpedo bomber crashed during a training exercise near Anacapa Island. The plane lies north of the gap between east and middle islands in about 120 feet of water and is a popular dive destination. (Photograph by Robert Schwemmer; NOAA.)

UNDERWATER WORLD AT ANACAPA ISLAND. Recreational scuba diving is a popular sport at Anacapa Island, where parts of the island offshore are set aside as marine protected areas, where taking of all living marine resources is prohibited. (Photograph by Dan Harding.)

CALIFORNIA SPINY LOBSTERS (*PANULIRUS INTERRUPTUS*). The underwater habitat around Anacapa Island is home to California spiny lobsters. They are nocturnal, hiding in crevices during the day, emerging at night to feed primarily on sea urchins, clams, mussels, and worms. Historically, they were commonly referred to as crawfish. (Photograph by Robert Schwemmer; NOAA.)

BLACK SEA BASS IN AN ANACAPA ISLAND KELP FOREST. Slow growth and reproduction of black sea bass, coupled with a tendency to aggregate in large groups, made these giants of the sea susceptible to overfishing. By the 1970s, they had become very rare. In 1982, both the recreational and commercial California fisheries for this species were closed, and as a result, giant sea bass are slowly recovering. (Photograph by Dan Harding.)

BLACK SEA BASS (*STEREOLEPIS GIGAS*) BREED OFF ANACAPA ISLAND. This gentle giant is the largest and most magnificent species of fish in the Anacapa Island kelp forests. Black sea bass are capable of growing to a length of over seven feet and a weight of up to 800 pounds. (Photograph by Jeff Bozanic.)

KAYAKING AT EAST ANACAPA ISLAND. East Anacapa Island is a kayaker's paradise. There are dozens of nearby coastal caves that can be easily accessed by kayak. Kayaks are transported to Landing Cove by Island Packers and offloaded on the lower dock. (Photograph by Dan Harding.)

KAYAKING IN CATHEDRAL COVE. Cathedral Cove, just west of Landing Cove, offers multiple caves that can be explored by kayak during calm seas. (SCIF.)

THE 12.2-MILE SWIM. Marathon swimming across the Santa Barbara Channel is a relatively new sport. It dates to the first documented Northern Channel Islands swim in 1978 by Cindy Cleveland, who swam to Anacapa Island and back. When swimming between Anacapa Island and the mainland, the single obvious point of reference for the marathon swimmer is an oil rig named Gina, four statute miles from Oxnard. (SBCSA.)

MARATHON SWIMMER LYNN KUBASEK, 2011. On October 21, 2011, Lynn Kubasek completed the 22nd successful swim-crossing from Anacapa Island to Oxnard. Assisted by a support team including Julie Flanagan in a kayak, Kubasek made the crossing in 67-to-68-degree water in just over seven hours. (SCIF; Lynn Kubasek.)

MAINLAND MARATHON SWIM ROUTE, ANACAPA ISLAND. Between 1978 and 2017, there have been 72 successful Channel swim crossings from Anacapa Island to the mainland—the preferred direction for swimming. Six people have swum in the opposite direction, from the mainland to Anacapa Island. Several swimmers have done the swim more than once. (SCIF; photograph by Bill Dewey.)

BURGEE OF THE ALL EIGHT CLUB, ESTABLISHED IN 1994. The flag's eight white stars, set in two groups, represent the four Northern and four Southern California Channel Islands. The All Eight Club was established in 1994 by the Santa Cruz Island Foundation to identify and honor those persons who have visited all eight California Channel Islands. To qualify, one must have walked on San Miguel, Santa Rosa, Santa Cruz, Anacapa, Santa Barbara, Santa Catalina, San Nicolas, and San Clemente islands. Access to San Nicolas and San Clemente islands is difficult due to their active military status. Members of the All Eight Club include biologists, anthropologists, botanists, ornithologists, zoologists, educators, helicopter and fixed wing pilots, a retired national park superintendent and park employee, a museum director, a lichenologist, a photographer, a retired judge, a sea captain, and a rock star. This is said to be the most exclusive recognized geographic club in the world, with membership in the low 200s—a tenth of the famous Seven Summits Club. (SCIF.)

www.ingramcontent.com/pod-product-compliance
Lightning Source LLC
Chambersburg PA
CBHW050922150426
42812CB00051B/1942